WRITE

to PROTECT *and* SERVE

A PRACTICAL GUIDE FOR WRITING BETTER POLICE REPORTS

JOHN CAGLE

UNG

UNIVERSITY *of*
NORTH GEORGIA
UNIVERSITY PRESS

Blue Ridge | Cumming | Dahlonega | Gainesville | Oconee

Published by:
University of North Georgia Press
Dahlonega, Georgia

Printing Support by:
Lightning Source Inc.
La Vergne, Tennessee

Cover image by Jordan Andrews.

Book design by Corey Parson.

ISBN: 978-1-940771-42-7

Printed in the United States of America.
For more information, please visit: http://ung.edu/university-press
or e-mail: ungpress@ung.edu.

CONTENTS

Chapter 1: The Importance of Writing Police Reports   1

Chapter 2: Uniform Crime Reporting   7

Chapter 3: Access to Reports and Our Audience   13

Chapter 4: Notetaking   21

Chapter 5: Formatting and Writing a Report   29

Chapter 6: Remembering Basic Grammar and Punctuation Rules 43

Chapter 7: Writing Reports That Contain More Action   61

Chapter 8: Compliance Writing   85

Chapter 9: Ethics in Writing   99

Chapter 10: A Look Back   109

Glossary   113

References   123

The Importance of Writing Police Reports

CHAPTER 1

DISCUSSION TOPIC

Each day across the United States, police officers and civilian personnel collect critical information about events that can have a significant impact on our lives. A house is burglarized, a car is stolen, someone is attacked or missing, and people are killed. If you have been a victim of a crime, you know first-hand how stressful it can be and how important a proper police response is. You expect officers to be timely, thorough, and well trained. Part of their training is learning the importance of collecting facts and how various partners in the criminal justice system use those facts.

CHAPTER LEARNING OBJECTIVES

- Recognize two types of police reports.
- Develop a clear understanding of the important reasons to do reports.
- Identify the agency responsible for collecting and tabulating certain crime data.
- Understand how time-consuming report writing can be.

Several years ago, the United States Army had a recruiting slogan: "Be All You Can Be." Around this nation, in big cities and small towns, another slogan appears on the side of marked police vehicles: "To Protect and Serve." Of course, that is the goal and should be the result of our actions. However, that is not the reason most people become interested in a job in the criminal justice field. I often ask students what caused them to become interested in a career in law enforcement, and their response is that they have a family member or friend who is on the job, or they have seen some cop show on television. First-hand knowledge of police work as actual work is not easy to obtain.

One television show can give us a glimpse into the real work this textbook discusses. That television show is from the 1960s and is called *Dragnet*. It was set in Los Angeles and followed two police detectives, Joe Friday and his partner Bill Gannon, as they solved crimes. They spend much of each episode interviewing witnesses or victims in order to catch the bad guy. Occasionally, you might see Bill taking notes in a small pocket notebook. If a witness got off track during the interview, Joe Friday would say, "Just the facts, ma'am." That is what report writing is all about: recording just the facts.

Today, the cop shows on television depict hard-core action. After all, that's what rakes in high ratings. However, as exciting—and at times realistic—as it may appear, that's just not real life. When I got into the business, I had no idea of the sheer volume of reports that are required. Report writing seems pretty far removed from the hard-core action scenes, but reports are the hard-core reality of police work. In fact, when asked what is the one thing officers dislike the most about their job, the answer is always "the paperwork."

Report writing is not sexy. It's not fun. It has no redeeming features other than being necessary. In order of priority, just under staying alive, the most important skill for a police officer is the ability to write a good report. When prosecutors are asked what they would like to see most from their police officers, almost all say better reports.

Good writing counts. When I go to one of those big box stores, I recall the time I was shopping for a new gas grill. Of course, the "manly" thing to do is buy the biggest, most expensive grill in the store. Those grills come with detailed instructions for assembly and often are hard to read and understand. Lack of attention to detail can lead to disaster. That is also true in report writing. Instructions are necessary; nevertheless, they are often given the short shrift. When I started in this business, the block of instruction on report writing was short. We all wanted to go to the firing range and the driving course, so we hurried through the writing and got back out to do things that were fun.

The process starts by learning this essential fact: To write a good report, we must understand why we do them in the first place. The main reason is to record the facts and circumstances

A police officer working on his computer in his patrol car.

of an event in a way that can be understood and preserved. As Joe Friday would say, "Just the facts." The reports do not read like novels trying to capture the attention of the reader; they should be accurate, complete, and brief—or as brief as they can be depending on the event. In other words, get to the point. Understanding the "why" can help us remember the importance of these reports. After all, we will spend a lot of time writing them. It is estimated that a patrol officer will spend half their time on shift writing reports. It's also estimated that detectives may spend as much as three-quarters of their time writing reports. Writing reports is a skill that must be learned properly. Developing bad habits in the beginning will only compound the difficulty of any attempts to improve later. You will undoubtedly encounter officers who have not developed their writing skills. You will also see firsthand that their reputation has consequently suffered both within the agency and the community. In today's modern criminal justice agencies, the lack of ability to write good reports is viewed as an indication of laziness. On the other hand, well-written reports are impressive and can serve as proof of professionalism and dedication. So, what is the "why?"

The "why's" are numerous. We write reports to refresh our memory at a later time about events that might've happened years ago. Prosecutors use the reports to make decisions about potential criminal charges. Reports allow supervisors to follow the progress of events to ensure that everything is complete. Agencies use reports to track crime trends and for use in strategic planning. This use, as well as reports that are completed describing incidents in the field, are referred to as external reports.

Internal reports are usually completed for administrative reasons. Examples of internal reports are training records, leave requests, use of force reports, commendations, press releases, inspection reports, and many others. One report that is commonly seen in jail settings is a log: cell count verification logs, medication logs, visitation logs, et cetera. Logs are the simplest form of reports and are relatively easy to learn to complete.

A detective typing up a report.

Another reason reports must be done is that every law enforcement agency in the United States is asked to report certain crime data to the Federal Bureau of Investigation. Each year, the FBI compiles and publishes the crime statistics. This report is essential in researching trends across the nation. It also gives an agency a look at others around them to determine local trends.

A note about this textbook: Unlike other textbooks on report writing that you may consult, this one does not contain limited practice writing exercises. In other books, the exercise information is delivered in written form. In other words, the facts about an event are already written down for you. They then convert that information into a narrative report. This form of delivery does not allow you to develop any kind of notetaking skills or style. Notetaking is critical because the skill is developed through practice. This book delivers all its writing exercises in a way that allows notetaking practice. This textbook also includes writing scenarios that represent realistic law-enforcement encounters.

DISCUSSION TOPIC REVIEW

- Name the two types of police reports and give examples of both.
- How are police reports used by prosecutors?
- What federal agency collects and tabulates crime data? How is it used?
- How can police agencies use information in reports to develop enforcement strategies?
- What are the estimates of time officers spend completing reports?

Uniform Crime Reporting

CHAPTER 2

DISCUSSION TOPIC

The International Association of Chiefs of Police (IACP) developed a system to report and record crime statistics. They wanted to provide law enforcement and regular citizens with a clear picture, or as clear as it could be, of the crimes that were being committed in the United States. In 1930, the United States Congress passed legislation authorizing the attorney general to begin collection of crime data. In turn, the attorney general designated the FBI to serve as the clearinghouse for that data. This system was named the Uniform Crime Reporting Program (UCR), or the Summary Reporting System (SRS). This system would collect, on a monthly basis, information from law enforcement agencies in the United States and be used to tabulate the frequency of certain crimes in local jurisdictions, states, and regions. Agencies submitted their crime data in written documents that were then hand entered into a computer system and analyzed. By 2003, the FBI compiled data from more than 16,000 agencies, which represents approximately 93% of the population.

Over the years, interest grew in developing more detailed crime data, and in 1988, another system within the Uniform

Crime Reporting Program was approved. It is called the National Incident-Based Reporting System or NIBRS. It collects information regarding more crime categories and can be electronically submitted. However, it is estimated that less than 50% of all law enforcement agencies submit crime information to this database.

CHAPTER LEARNING OBJECTIVES

- Identify the crimes tracked by the Uniform Crime Reporting Program's Summary Reporting System (SRS).
- Identify the crimes tracked by the National Incident-Based Reporting System (NIBRS).
- Demonstrate the ability to recognize and complete the forms used to collect crime data for these systems.

The IACP identified the crimes they believed were the most important to track. They divided the crimes into two categories: Part I and Part II offenses. Part I crimes are known as index crimes and are considered more serious than are those in Part II. All other criminal offenses, except traffic offenses, are called Part II.

Part I

Violent crimes:

- Murder
- Forcible Rape
- Robbery
- Aggravated Assault

Property crimes:

- Arson
- Burglary

- Larceny/theft
- Motor vehicle theft

Part II

- Simple assault
- Curfew offenses and loitering
- Embezzlement
- Forgery and counterfeiting
- Disorderly conduct
- Driving under the influence
- Drug offenses
- Fraud
- Gambling
- Liquor offenses
- Offenses against the family
- Prostitution
- Public drunkenness
- Runaways
- Sex offenses
- Stolen property
- Vandalism
- Vagrancy
- Weapon offenses

Data for Part I is collected using reported crimes. Data for Part II is collected from arrests made for those crimes. Once a crime is reported, certain information is collected for use with the UCR. This information includes, but is not limited to, the type of crime, the date and time of the crime, the location or jurisdiction, victim information, offender information (if available), value of property stolen or recovered, type of weapon used (if applicable), any drugs that may be involved, and whether or not the event was cleared by an arrest or closed administratively.

The National Incident-Based Reporting System collects information using two offense categories called Group A and Group B. This system collects more detailed information about a wider variety of crimes. The Summary Reporting System used what came to be known as the "Hierarchy Rule" to determine what offense was tracked. Let's take, for instance, someone robbing a bank and during the robbery, the teller was murdered. Using the "Hierarchy Rule," the more serious offense (murder) takes precedence and would be reported over the lesser offense (robbery). Offenders frequently commit several crimes during a single event, and NIBRS collects data on all offenses committed during the incident.

Group A

- Animal cruelty
- Arson
- Aggravated assault
- Bribery
- Burglary
- Counterfeiting
- Destruction/damage to property
- Drug/narcotic offenses
- Embezzlement
- Extortion/blackmail
- Fraud
- Gambling
- Homicide
- Human trafficking
- Kidnapping
- Larceny
- Motor vehicle theft
- Pornography
- Prostitution

- Robbery
- Sex offenses, forcible
- Sex offenses, non-forcible
- Stolen property offenses
- Weapons violations

Group B

- Bad checks
- Curfew/vagrancy violations
- Disorderly conduct
- Driving under the influence
- Drunkenness
- Family offenses, nonviolent
- Liquor law violations
- Peeping Tom
- Runaway
- Trespass

This information is available to everyone, and some cities use it for marketing as well. If a city is trying to sponsor a large event such as the World Series or Super Bowl, they might examine the crime rate in that area and compare it to other cities vying for the same event. I suspect that the planners for the Olympic Games in Atlanta looked at this information and used it for their bid to host in 1996.

Officers in the field collect all the essential information about these crimes and document the information in their reports. Report writing is often the first movement of the so-called "wheels" of justice in the criminal justice system and mark the beginning of the road to the resolution of criminal events. Open the link below and look at your state and local crime information. Compare it to other jurisdictions of similar size. Examples of forms used to collect the crime data described above are contained at this site under the "Data Collection" section: https://ucr.fbi.gov.

DISCUSSION TOPIC REVIEW

- What agency developed the Uniform Crime Reporting Program?
- Why are crime statistics collected?
- Name the two databases used to collect and tabulate crime data. What are their differences?
- Whose responsibility is it to transmit crime data?

Access to Reports and Our Audience

CHAPTER 3

DISCUSSION TOPIC

The trial of O. J. Simpson should serve notice to all that during a criminal proceeding, a common strategy of defense lawyers is *attack the police when all else fails.* Those of us who watched the trial on television may conclude that some of the basis for the attacks that the police underwent might have been self-incurred. When mistakes are made, the defense will highlight those mistakes when discovered. Technical mistakes regarding the law or certain operational mistakes, such as a failure to properly collect evidence, are the ones we hear the most about. However, mistakes in reports can cause problems too. Those mistakes can be particularly embarrassing because reports are frequently released to the public. Below is a transcript of a potential courtroom encounter between an officer who made mistakes in their report and a defense lawyer.

Question: Now detective, you have written in your report that the date this offense occurred was June 1, 2012. We all know that the date this offense occurred was June 3, 2012. I assume this was just a mistake on your part in the report?

Answer: Yes, sir.

Question: Now detective, in your report you described my client as approximately 6'2" tall. I have asked my client to stand up next to me, and I will state detective that I am 5'10" tall, and ask you to note that my client is shorter than me. I assume, detective, that this was another simple mistake in your report?

Answer: Yes, sir.

Question: In your report, detective, you indicated that you arrived on the scene at 12:30 p.m. and began the search. I show you an evidence receipt which indicates that you began your search at 1:30 p.m. Just what time did you begin your search, detective?

Answer: The search started at 12:30 p.m.

Question: Can you explain why there are two different times in your report indicating when the search started?

Answer: It was a typo in the report.

Question: During your direct testimony, you stated that my client told you that he shot the victim. I hand you your report, detective, and ask you to show me where in your report you documented that statement?

Answer: It's not in my report, but he said it.

Question: I show you a copy of a property receipt completed by you regarding the recovery of five 38-caliber shell casings during your search. The property receipt states you placed the shell casings in a plastic bag. I hold the plastic evidence bag and show you that it contains four 38-caliber shell casings. Where is the other shell casing, detective?

Answer: I think I only recovered four.

Question: So that is a mistake in your report?

Answer: Yes.

Question: Detective, please look in your file which you have with you on the stand and look at the transcript of the tape-recorded statement made by my client.

Answer: There is no transcript.

Question: Since there is no transcript, please get the CD containing the recording of the statement my client made.

Answer: There is no recording.

Question: I show you, detective, a copy of an inventory of your issued equipment. It indicates that you are currently issued three digital recorders. Please tell the jury, detective, why you did not record this so-called statement.

Answer: I just did not think it was necessary.

Question: You say in your report that the offense occurred on June 1, but we now know that is a mistake. You completed a two-page report. I call your attention to the date at the end of your report and ask you what that means? January 5, 2013.

Answer: That's when the report was completed and typed.

Question: Can you tell the jury why it took almost eight months to complete a two-page report?

Answer: I was busy with other cases.

Question: I show you a copy of your handwritten notes that were provided to me by the prosecutor. How long are these notes, detective?

Answer: About one paragraph.

Question: So your entire testimony today and your two-page report is a summation of one paragraph of notes.

Answer: Yes.

Speaker: So ladies and gentlemen of the jury, the state would ask that you believe the testimony of this detective even though his report contains many errors, it was prepared eight months after the event, there appears to be missing evidence, and, even though he is issued three digital recorders, there is no recording or transcript of the alleged statements my client supposedly made. I submit that his entire testimony is not worthy of belief and that it should be disregarded in its entirety.

CHAPTER LEARNING OBJECTIVES

- Identify who can obtain police reports.
- Learn the basis for which state and local governments must disclose public documents.
- Recognize errors in police reports that can affect the outcome of witness testimony.

We have discussed why we write reports. We should also consider who will have access to the reports once they're written.

"Who" is just about everybody: lawyers, suspects, the media, victims, insurance companies, and other police agencies. These days, it's not that uncommon to find a copy of our reports on the front-page of the newspaper or on the Internet.

Almost every state and, of course, the federal government has a law requiring the disclosure of certain government documents. It's usually called an open records law or Freedom of Information Act (FOIA). Here is an example of the first paragraph of Georgia's law:

> The General Assembly finds and declares that the strong public policy of the state is in favor of open government; that open government is essential to free, open, and democratic society; and that public access to public records should be encouraged to foster confidence in government and so that the public can evaluate the expenditure of public funds and the efficient and proper functioning of its institutions. The General Assembly further finds and declares that there is a strong presumption that public records should be made available for public inspection without delay. (Open Records Act, O.C.G.A. § 50-18-70, 2010.)

This law means that since our agencies are part of the government, our reports are too. We are not only required to provide our documents, but also are required to do so within a very short window of time. Attachments (such as photographs, sketches, crime lab reports, and tape recordings) must be disclosed as well. Occasionally, however, our reports have content that may be exempt from disclosure. Such exemptions may include things like the names of juveniles (unless one is being tried in court as an adult) the names of victims of sexual assault, the identifying data and addresses of police officers (unless they are the subject of an investigation), autopsies, and some crime scene reports to name a few. I strongly suggest you become familiar with the open records laws in your particular state because it is important to know what must be released, and it is just as important to know what should not be released.

Our audience is broad. That is why we must take great care to ensure reports are completed properly. Police reports must contain all facts and circumstances about an event known at the time. They should not be vague or leave the reader wondering why critical information was not obtained. Below, you will see a short report regarding a theft. Read this report and identify information that you believe should be included but has been omitted. In other words, what's missing?

On April 16, 2016, at approximately 9:00 a.m., I (Officer Bill Smith) was dispatched to take a theft report. I arrived at the address and spoke with the homeowner. He stated that he lives at that address with his wife and two children. He and his family left for vacation and came back home at about 8 o'clock that morning (April 16). When he got home, he noticed that his riding lawnmower was not there. I obtained the serial number for the lawnmower, and he said it is valued at eight hundred dollars ($800.00).

I walked behind his house, and he showed me the area where the lawnmower had been stored. I was able to see tire tracks leading from that area through the backyard and into a wooded area behind the home. I photographed the tire tracks. No other tire tracks were seen in the backyard or in the woods. No additional information was obtained from the homeowner.

Now listen to the audio file that provides more details of this event, and see how many of your questions are answered. You will write your own report about this incident in a later chapter.

Theft Report

https://web.ung.edu/media/university-press/write-protect-serve-audio/theft.m4a

DISCUSSION TOPIC REVIEW

- Identify errors made by the detective in the report referenced in the transcript. Remember, the reports the detective relied upon during this proceeding contain no information that would be excluded from an open records request.
- Are you able to see clearly how mistakes can cause stress for the detective during his testimony?
- How might a badly-written report affect the outcome of a criminal proceeding?
- Were most of your concerns resolved by the additional information provided in the theft audio file?

Notetaking

CHAPTER 4

DISCUSSION TOPIC

Watch and listen to this episode of *Dragnet* title, "The Big Thief." Take notes of the details of this event.

CHAPTER LEARNING OBJECTIVES

- Understand the importance of taking good field notes.
- Learn the supplies needed to take notes.
- Develop one's own style of taking notes.
- Understand the need to proofread and edit reports.
- Recall specific details depicted in "The Big Thief."

There are three stages of every police report. It starts with collecting content (facts) about an event, then organizing notes and writing the report itself, and proofreading and editing the final document.

Content

Learning the facts usually starts with interviewing a victim or witness, or seeing something unfold in front of us. That's where we find information such as the who, what, when, where, and how (4W+H) of events that we should include in all reports. Most of your concerns in the theft report in the previous chapter were likely content omissions. Let's examine them. The homeowner's name was missing (the who). The exact date when the family left to go on vacation was missing (the when). The brand name, a description, and serial number of the lawn mower was missing (the what). The homeowner's address and location where the lawnmower had been stored was missing (the where). It was noted, however, that lawnmower tire tracks were seen heading toward the woods (the how). Of course, all of this information is important and must be collected and documented.

There will be events that are more complicated and may cause each of these "content" sections to become lengthy. For instance, an interview with a victim of an assault must go into great detail regarding the description of the offender to include sex, race, height, weight, hair color and length, facial hair (if any), distinguishing marks or tattoos, and clothing description (the who). Specific details of the attack need to include weapons used (if any), statements made by the offender, and a complete description of each injury sustained by the victim (the how). I think you get the idea. Some events are more serious than others; therefore, documenting the who, what, when, where, and how will need a great deal of attention.

Organizing Notes and Writing the Report

We are all human. We forget things. Many times throughout the day, officers learn certain details of suspected criminal activity and the only way to remember them all is to write them down. Learning to take good notes is the first step in report writing. You need to make sure that you always have available the proper tools and supplies for taking notes. Now, this is not rocket science. I'm talking about a simple notepad and pen. In order to collect all the information needed, officers must have sufficient supplies on hand that meet their needs for any situation. By supplies, I mean multiple notebooks, pens, business cards, Miranda cards, forms, recorders, and even cameras. Most investigators use what is called a portfolio binder. These contain storage compartments and allow for quick access to these supplies. They are a good way to organize materials in a professional-looking manner.

Most patrol officers carry a small notebook in their uniform shirt pocket. This type of notebook should only be used to write down information such as a tag number, a phone number, or a name. They are not sufficient to write down details of an event. Certainly, patrol officers should not be expected to approach cars at a traffic stop holding a notebook, but they should have one available in their car. Some suggest that pens with black ink are the best to use when taking notes because black ink will last longer. I agree, but my position has always been that I would rather have something written in crayon than nothing written at all.

Take notes so that you can make sense of them. When interviewing someone and taking notes, you control the pace of the interview. You have the ability to stop at any time to ask for clarification of facts or even how to spell something. Don't get in a hurry. Develop your own style of notetaking. By style, I mean the ability to organize the information on the page in a manner that will allow you to use it later in order to complete the report more efficiently. You should cover simple things, such as remembering that every report must note the date and time. Also, notes must be legible—not necessarily legible to someone else, but certainly to you. There are occasions when you are required to maintain or keep your rough notes before a court proceeding. I suggest that once you fill up a notebook, write the date range somewhere on it. Doing so will help you recover it easily if you had to. You should not write personal messages, personal phone numbers, or other personal notes on your business notepad just in case you have to provide it to the prosecutor or others. Your notebook will also likely contain notes pertaining to different events. Each event is issued a unique case number; therefore, beginning your notes of that event with that case number is essential. These case numbers, sometimes called file numbers, are issued by the agency.

One thing that will keep you on track while preparing the report is organizing your notes first. Make an outline of the topics you need to cover. Inevitably, during an interview with a victim or witness, they will think of something that relates to what you wrote down on page one. Now you're on page ten. Remember, our reports should describe events in chronological order, and that's how you should do your interview. However, sometimes your notes don't turn out like that. When reviewing your notes, I suggest you develop a system that you can use to organize your thoughts. I would always try to review my notes and place a number by a sentence containing a topic that I thought should go at a certain place in my report. If my notes consisted of five pages, there would usually be some information out of chronological order. During an interview, there are often multiple topics discussed, so organizing the report by topic is a must. If at the beginning of the report you write about injuries to the victim, and in the middle of the report you write about injuries to the victim, and then more injuries are discussed toward the end of the report, you will lose the reader's attention. Finish all the facts about one topic before going to the next. That is why the numbering system worked for me. Many times, especially for follow-up investigations, detectives' notes might consist of twenty or thirty pages. That is another reason to come up with a system that you can use when preparing your report, so it will tell the story the way it must be told. Covering all the "number one's" before going to "number two's"—and placing a line over them as you go—will ensure that you write about every topic in your notes. Doing so can speed things up at the end. Once each paragraph of your notes is crossed out, you're through with the report.

Proofreading and Editing

Once you have completed writing the report, check it for errors and correct them. I suggest you follow this simple outline:

1. Does the report comply with agency formatting guidelines? In other words, does it look like it should? Most agencies have specific requirements, such as the use of first-person vs. third-person sentences or military vs. civilian reporting times. Some agencies have specific requirements as to font size and spacing. After writing a few reports, such requirements will become easy to remember.

2. Ensure that the report is grammatically correct. Remember, this report and the way you write it reflects on you and your agency. Misspelled words and improper use of punctuation must be corrected. Most writing software contains programs that can help you identify these errors as the report is being completed. However, you should not rely on this software totally. Take your time and read each line with a sharp eye for errors.

3. Look for any omissions of required "content." That's the 4W+H information. If any of this information is missing, you should attempt to recover it. This might involve a simple phone call to a victim or witness to follow up on an earlier interview.

4. Make sure the report properly tells the story in a way that can be easily followed and understood by everyone. If it sounds confusing to you, it will most certainly sound confusing to others.

5. Don't worry if you struggle in the beginning. Before you submit a report, have a trusted colleague review it and offer

suggestions and feedback. This will increase your confidence level for future reports.

The objective here is to develop your skills to a degree where you feel comfortable and confident writing reports. Preventing reports from being kicked back by supervisors due to errors should be your goal. Writing the same report many times over should be avoided.

DISCUSSION TOPIC REVIEW

Below are questions relating to facts contained in the *Dragnet* episode. Search your notes for the answers.

Dragnet, "The Big Thief"

https://web.ung.edu/media/university-press/write-protect-serve-audio/dragnet.mp4

Dragnet Video Questions

"The Big Thief"

1. In what city did the crime occur?

2. On what date did the first crime occur?

3. What are the names of the two detectives assigned to the robbery case?

4. What is the name of the first doctor who was robbed?

5. What was the location of the hotel where the first robbery occurred?

6. What items were stolen from the first robbery victim?

7. What was the alias used by the robbery suspect?

8. What was the address where the shooting took place?

9. How old was the suspect who was shot and killed by the detective?

Here are the answers. Compare them to your notes. How did you do?

1. In what city did the crime occur?
   Los Angeles, California

2. On what date did the first crime occur?
   Wednesday, June 17

3. What are the names of the two detectives assigned to the robbery case?
   Frank Smith and Joe Friday

4. What is the name of the first doctor who was robbed?
   Dr. Aaron R. Platt

5. What was the location of the hotel where the first robbery occurred?
   At the corner of Pembroke and Columbia

6. What items were stolen from the first robbery victim?
   Watch, wallet, solid gold lighter, narcotics

7. What was the alias used by the robbery suspect?
   Timothy Allen

8. What was the address where the shooting took place?
   9276 South Dixon

9. How old was the suspect who was shot and killed by the detective?

22 years old

This exercise illustrates the need to take good notes. If you don't write it down in a way that makes sense to you, you will not remember details when it's time to do the report.

Formatting and Writing a Report

CHAPTER 5

DISCUSSION TOPIC

Decisions about how reports look largely rest with individual agencies. The use of first-person or third-person sentences or reporting time (using military or civilian methods) are additional choices for agencies. Spacing, font size, margins and the use of agency letterhead are considerations as well. Most agencies have purchased record management systems (RMS) to aid in report writing. This technology enhances the ability to link information contained in reports with other critical information collected and stored.

Officers usually prepare police reports based on the chronological order of the event. Therefore, the first thing officers say is, "Start at the beginning and tell me what happened."

In the audio files below, the speaker is giving details to an officer about a theft, a burglary, and a neighborhood canvass. Take notes as you listen. Avoid pausing the audio file.

Theft Report

https://web.ung.edu/media/university-press/write-protect-serve-audio/theft.m4a

Burglary Report

https://web.ung.edu/media/university-press/write-protect-serve-audio/burglary.m4a

Neighborhood Canvass Report

https://web.ung.edu/media/university-press/write-protect-serve-audio/neighborhood-canvass-report.m4a

CHAPTER LEARNING OBJECTIVES

- Develop a clear understanding of agency requirements for writing.
- Demonstrate the ability to write sentences using first-person and third-person.
- Demonstrate the ability to convert civilian time into military time.
- Understand the difference between active and passive writing.
- Understand the function of records management systems.
- Demonstrate the ability to take notes well.
- Demonstrate the ability to write narrative reports of the events described in the three audio files.

A Discussion of Forms

Agencies in the criminal justice system have been and will always be form driven. For almost every task, a form has to be completed: forms for training requests, use of force, arrest reports, Miranda waivers, consent to search, and incident reports to name a few. In agencies with record management systems, vendors will load the forms into the software by the vendor. For instance, in the training module, all forms about training will be found there.

In the human resource module, everything from employment application forms to exit interview forms can be found. Report writing modules contain all forms necessary to complete reports. Such organization is crucial.

Some forms are agency specific. That is to say, the agency designs the form so it can be easily recognized. The use of letterhead or name is usually part of the design.

Forms used by agencies usually have several purposes. Forms can provide a guide to collect information. They prompt the writer by asking for information such as DOB, sex, address, and the date. These forms often contain information about specific crimes, victims of crimes, and the offender. Most forms have simple fill-in-the-blanks or blocks to add information. Since the inception of records management systems, these forms have evolved and have become easier to complete. For example, an RMS vendor can upload the names of the crimes in your state, along with the corresponding criminal code numbering system. An example might be "Theft, 16.8.14." If an officer were taking a report of a theft, the form would have a block to record the name of the crime. The officer can configure the form using a drop box, selecting from choices in the drop box to complete that section. Some electronic forms will not allow you to move to another section until you complete the required fields. This capability is an advantage we did not have previously to ensure we collected and documented all information.

A form was created to fill the need to gather crime information and report it to the FBI. The report is identified by many different names throughout the nation, but the one most commonly used is an incident report. Some agencies refer to it as a Face Page. These forms can be modified to collect other information and data that the FBI does not require.

Consider an example of an incident report included here: The Watkinsville Police Department Incident Report. It is a typical incident report collecting UCR data. Some information, such as case numbers and agency identifiers, are agency specific. Other parts are completed based on facts the officers obtain from victims, offenders, and suspects, as well as values of property stolen or recovered. The report also notes the status of the event, such as whether it is active, cleared by arrest, unfounded, or administratively cleared.

The responding officer usually completes the incident report form about an event, collecting the initial information and data. For instance, an officer responds to a theft or a burglary. They arrive, gather necessary information, and complete the incident report. When that report is reviewed, it is typically assigned to an investigator who continues the investigation. The investigator completes any follow-up reports on that event. To identify these reports, the investigator will use the same case number they had in the beginning.

In this discussion of an incident report form, we have been prompted to collect data by filling in blanks or blocks with the information we have received. However, as you work your way through the form, you will eventually come to a section routinely called "Narrative." The narrative is where officers write the facts and circumstances of the event. Describing the who, where, what, when, and how takes the most time to complete and is where most officers struggle.

Times

Most of the events occur in a sequence of time. For example, a person who arrives at a liquor store enters the store at a particular time, takes certain actions in sequence while they are inside, and then leaves. Usually, these things have already occurred before officers get there. Following a robbery, officers probably ask the store clerk to tell them what happened. That means for the clerk to start at the beginning and give the details of the robbery as it occurred. Words such as *entered*, *told*, *took*, and *left* are used most commonly to describe what happened. These words are examples of past tense. In the following example, notice the difference in past tense and present tense.

> *The store clerk said the robber enters the store at 11 a.m. He tells me to lie down on the floor. He takes the money from the register and leaves.*

That is an example of statements using the present tense.

> *The store clerk said the robber entered the store at 11 a.m. He told the clerk to lie down on the floor. He took the money from the register and left the store.*

That is an example of statements using past tense. Most reports you write should be past tense.

Remember that everything happens at a particular time. You arrive at a scene at a certain time, you stop a car at a certain time, criminals go about their business of committing crimes at certain times, and we interview victims, witnesses, and suspects at certain times. Therefore, the times these events take place is critical and must be documented. Occasionally during an interview with a victim or witness, you will be given a time when something happened based on an action they took. For example, a victim might tell you they had just looked at their watch, and it was about 2:00 p.m. when an event took place. That information is important to document as it helps determine the beginning of the sequence of events.

Almost everyone carries or wears a watch these days. However, rarely is everyone's watch exactly in sync with others. Therefore, when documenting time in your reports, you should use the word *approximately*. We should always try to get as close to the exact time something happens, but sometimes that's just not possible.

Many different "times" are used in the world today: Eastern Standard Time, Mountain Time, and Central Standard Time are a few. No matter where you are, you will use one of two methods to report times: military time and civilian time. The use of military time removes the need for a.m. or p.m. because military time uses the numeral hours in a day. The first hour of the day in military time looks like 0100 and is commonly recorded as 0100 hrs. One o'clock in the afternoon is recorded as 1300 hrs. This numbering system continues until 2400 hrs., which is midnight in civilian time.

Civilian time is what most of us outside the military use. The use of civilian time must include a.m. or p.m. Just writing 1 o'clock in a report is unclear. Don't assume that the reader will understand what time it is unless you use a.m. or p.m.

Active vs. Passive Voice

In a sentence with active voice, the subject is doing the action verb and the noun phrase in the predicate (everything after the verb) is receiving the action.

> _The man_ stole **the money**. What was stolen? **The money**. Who stole the money? _The man_.

In a sentence with passive voice, the object receiving the action is in the subject, and the object doing the action is in the predicate.

> **The money** _was stolen by_ _the man_. What was stolen? **The money**. Who stole the money? _The man_.

The following example uses a linking verb. It links a description in the predicate to the noun in the subject. Linking verbs are neither active or passive; they're only descriptive.

> _The driver of the car was impaired._ The driver = impaired

The following sentences are more examples of passive voice If the sentence is passive, you should be able to add "by John Doe" at the end.

The crime was committed on January 3rd <u>by John Doe</u>.
The house was broken into.
The suspect was shot by the witness.
The witnesses were questioned.

If you don't have specific details, you might have to settle for the passive voice.

Steve Smith was shot.

This sentence uses passive voice since the shooter is unknown. Nevertheless, it identifies Steve Smith as the person who was shot. Our reports are best written in active voice because it makes clear who the actors are. The following sentences use active voice.

<u>The driver, Mary Smith</u>, failed **the field Breathalyzer exam.**

Who failed the test? The driver. This sentence gives the name of the driver as well as the sobriety test that she failed.

Karen Crane stated she could identify the suspect.

The sentence provides the identity of the witness who can identify the suspect. If you have complete information, you should include it in each sentence of your report.

On Monday, June 2, 2016, the detective arrested John Jones and charged him with burglary.

This sentence provides the date, who made the arrest, the name of the person arrested, and the specific charge.

First-Person vs. Third-Person

The decision to use first-person or third-person point of view rests with your agency. Most federal law enforcement agencies still write in third-person. The agency I worked for did; therefore, that is how I was trained. It becomes easier the more you do it.

Third-person point of view uses specific names and pronouns to refer to each person, regardless of who the speaker is.

On the morning of April 10, 2016, **Detective John Smith** *arrived at 64 Main St. to investigate a robbery.* **He** *arrived at the bank at 9:37 a.m.*

An agency may prefer first-person sentences. They are sometimes easier to read and follow. First-person writing uses the pronouns *I* and *me*. The author must be who the *I* refers to.

On the morning of April 10, 2016, **I** *arrived at 64 Main St. to investigate a robbery.* **I** *arrived at the bank at 9:37 a.m.*

First-person reporting can be a little confusing if not done properly. The sentence above assumes the reader knows who the *I* is. If there has been no mention of the identity of the author, I suggest you use the following language during the first sentence of the report:

On the morning of April 10, 2016, **I (Detective John Smith)** *arrived at 64 Main St. to investigate a robbery. I arrived at the bank at 9:37 a.m.*

It becomes clear in this sentence which detective arrived at the scene. From then on, the use of the word *I* alone is acceptable in the report.

Identity

Somewhere in the report, you must identify everyone you talk with during an event. Some forms have a specific place to list what I call ID data. This information consists of a full name, date of birth or age, address, and contact telephone numbers. Some agencies also collect email addresses. On forms lacking a clear ID data section, list this information at the end of the narrative report, down a left column. Here is an example:

ID data:
Jerry Jones
White male
DOB: October 4, 1958
421 Elm Street, Clearlake, South Carolina, 46120
Telephone number: 803-555-7234

Jargon

Report writing needs accuracy. Our reports should be brief and to the point whenever possible. We cannot sacrifice accuracy in the name of brevity, but we should take advantage of opportunities that will help complete these reports quickly.

Diction, or word choice, is important. Jargon is diction specialized to a particular profession or group. We often use jargon while talking to each other since it saves time when we and others in the profession already understand it. In our business, we often hear words such as *BOLO* (be on the lookout) and *DOA* (dead on arrival) and phrases such as *bad guy* (suspect) or *drop a dime* (call). I can still remember the first time I heard someone say,

"Let's drop a dime on the bad guy." I had no idea what we were about to do. Most people outside the profession wouldn't either, so avoid the use of jargon unless you clarify what it means.

Be Thorough

In our reports, we must describe everything that we are told and what we do, see, and hear. The goal of any criminal investigation is to leave no stone unturned. The same goes for report writing. Document everything you do. For example, in an investigation of murder in a home, you conduct a crime scene search. You go room to room describing what you see, collecting evidence, and photographing potential evidence. You will most likely enter rooms that do not contain any items of evidentiary value. You must describe that fact in your report. If you attempted to locate latent fingerprints at a scene but were unsuccessful, you must report that. If you conducted a field test of something you believed was bloodstained but turned out not to be, you must report it. The narrative report about this crime scene search would contain multiple descriptions of activities that were not helpful in the investigation. But think about the audience again. If you did not describe each room in the house and whether or not you found any evidence in those rooms, your report would not be thorough. A goal for your investigation and report writing should be to never hear the question, *"Did you do _____?"*

Another example of being thorough is an interview-based investigative technique, commonly used during follow-up investigations, called a neighborhood canvass. In a neighborhood canvass, you talk to the neighbors to see if they saw anything. You will, however, speak with some who did not see anything or were not home during the event. Do we have to write a report about those who didn't see anything? Yes. Again, remember who our audience is. If you made an arrest in this case, the prosecutor would review the file to prepare for court. If you did not document the fact that you conducted a neighborhood canvass, even though it did not produce any results, you might be accused of doing a sloppy investigation. A report about a neighborhood canvass can be very easy to complete, especially in the event none of the neighbors had any information. One report describing all your contacts with neighbors is the best approach.

As a supervisor, I reviewed a report a detective prepared regarding a recorded interview. The report started like this:

On January 10, 1998, Detective Joe Smith interviewed Clarence Jones. See attached transcript.

The transcript attached to this report was fifty-seven pages long. As the reader, I had to read the entire manuscript in order to know what Clarence Jones said. On page fifty of the transcript, Jones confessed to the crime. I had to read fifty pages of "how to make a watch" before I got to the point. That's not the way to write a report. Because this detective was lazy, he did not want to review the audio/video recordings to prepare a summation of what was said. That's what he should have done, though.

During a sit-down interview, you as the interviewer need to pay attention to what they say and what they look like when they say it. You probably won't use your notetaking skills during these types of interviews. While you should be prepared by having your pen and notepad available, you will sometimes find it's more important just to sit back and listen, knowing the recorder is capturing everything. During a thirty-minute interview, you might take a few notes, but not enough to prepare the report. Preparing it will therefore require you to review the audio/video recording and take notes from that. As you work your way through the interview, you will have the luxury of stopping the recording anytime you need to do so. Your note-taking style will not change. Inevitably, sections of the interview will be irrelevant. Don't waste your time writing about those. Remember: just the facts. Even though the transcript of the interview I mentioned was fifty-seven pages long, the report or summation of that interview—that I required the detective to complete—was only three pages long. On some occasions, these types of reports can certainly be very lengthy, but always use technology as an advantage during report writing. If the encounter is limited, your notes will be brief. You must always review these recordings as you complete your report. If your written report does not match the audio/video recordings, you will suffer the consequences later. More agencies are purchasing body-worn cameras for their officers. The ability to review these recordings in a timely manner in order to complete reports will, I believe, be a challenge.

Details

As you go about your business talking to people and collecting information, you will sometimes be tempted to hand a witness or suspect a notepad and say, "Write your statement." If your agency requires you to do this, then you must. If it is not necessary, then you should avoid this practice. Inevitably, witnesses will not write about specific details they saw or heard unless you prompt them to do so. Furthermore, suspects always minimize their activities to reduce their involvement in a crime. But what should you do when there are twenty bank robbery witnesses to interview? Think priorities. The most important witness will certainly be the person who had the most contact with the robber. This will likely be the teller. Regarding priority, you should interview the teller first. What about the other nineteen witnesses? While you are talking with the teller, you could have the other witnesses write down what they saw or heard, if anything. However, an officer should review their statements to make sure they report all relevant information. You can use their handwritten notes to prepare the official version of their recollections about the crime.

When interrogating suspects, on the other hand, I recommend that you never rely solely on something witnesses wrote down during the interrogation. If they do write out a statement, you must review it with them to ensure it discusses the who, what, when, where, and how of the event.

All of these categories require details. Reporting specific details is critical. You should, however, avoid giving your opinion or making an assumption in your reports. For instance, a statement in your report says, *"The suspect seemed intoxicated."* The word *seemed* is an assumption. Substantiate such observations with specific details A better way to write it would be, *"The suspect seemed intoxicated because he could not speak clearly."*

We must be very specific and avoid using vague words. Consider a sentence stating, *"Ralph Jones acted aggressively toward the officer."* This sentence is inappropriate because it does not specifically describe the actions that Ralph Jones is taking which causes him to appear aggressive. A better statement would be, *"Ralph Jones was fighting with the officer."*

I reviewed a crime scene report years ago about a woman who was murdered in her home. The crime scene investigator described the victim's wounds and stated: *"The victim died immediately from her wounds."* This statement is inappropriate because the investigator assumed the victim died immediately. He could not possibly know at what point the victim died. A more appropriate statement would be, *"The victim died in the bedroom."*

You can have these opinions, but you should avoid writing them in a report unless you specifically state the reason why. Again, use clear and specific words. You should avoid sentences such as:

The witness was hostile. What does "hostile" mean?

The suspect was nervous. What was the suspect doing which caused them to appear nervous?

He was probably involved in the crime. What facts do you have to form that opinion?

The defendant looked scared. What specific actions displayed by the defendant caused them to appear scared?

The neighbor had a bad attitude. What was the neighbor doing which caused you to think they had a bad attitude?

A window was found broken in the garage door (point of entry). The point of entry is an assumption not based on fact. A way to correct this sentence would be, *"There was a broken window in the garage (possible point of entry)."*

DISCUSSION TOPIC REVIEW

- Look at the transcripts of the audio file regarding the theft, burglary, and neighborhood canvass. Compare them to your notes to make sure you wrote down all the details.
- Identify the 4W+H of each event along with any other information you think would be relevant to collect.
- Write a narrative report describing the events of each incident. Alternate using first-person vs. third-person, and military vs. civilian time.

Remembering Basic Grammar and Punctuation Rules

CHAPTER 6

DISCUSSION TOPIC

In the first and second grade, most of us learned to read and write. We also began to spell simple words. As our education continued, we learned how to write sentences that made sense. Those of us who went to college had to write lengthy research papers, too. We found nouns, verbs, adjectives, and adverbs all over the place. Our sentences included commas, periods, semicolons, apostrophes, and question marks. Some of us have remembered those things better than others. Therefore, a quick review of these topics is in order.

Sentence: a set of words that is a complete statement, typically containing a subject and a verb. It conveys a statement, question, exclamation, or command, and consists of a main clause and sometimes one or more subordinate clauses.

CHAPTER LEARNING OBJECTIVES

- Recall basic writing rules as they relate to punctuation, grammar, sentence structure, and spelling.

Even the definition of a sentence can get a little complicated, but I will endeavor to keep this discussion as simple as I can. You should not expect to have a report kicked back to you with a sticky note identifying grammar problems with your sentences, stating, for example, *dangling participle*. That just won't happen. The key in writing sentences is to keep them as simple as you can. Choosing words that we all know and understand, and using the basic punctuation rules and correct spelling will help do that.

One of the biggest problems I've seen in police reports is trying to pack too much information into one sentence. As we review our notes in preparation for the final report, we often see long lists of information and statements. In an attempt to shorten them, we combine topics that, when written together, just don't make sense. I can remember reading a court decision document, the first sentence of which covered half a page. It had a lot of punctuation, which I'm sure was correct, but I'd forgotten what the topic was by the time I got to the end. A rule to remember: If you have to reread it, something is wrong with it.

Pronoun Antecedents

To be complete, sentences need a subject and verb. The subject is a noun: a thing, a person, or a pronoun. When a pronoun is used, the antecedent must be clear: Who does *he/she/it* refer to? Remember that our reports must tell the whole story about an event. Sentences that don't identify pronoun-antecedent fail to tell the whole story because they are not clear.

*<u>John</u> saw <u>the man</u> shoot at the police, and **he** ran across the street to report it.*

Who ran to make the report: John or the man? Clarify the pronoun:

*<u>John</u> saw <u>the man</u> shoot at the police, and **John** ran across the street to report it.*

*<u>Barbara</u> saw <u>the girl</u> being attacked, and **she** ran for help.*

*<u>Barbara</u> saw <u>the girl</u> being attacked, and **she (Barbara)** ran for help.*

Make sure that each sentence is accurate, describes all the actors and their actions, and leaves nothing for interpretation.

Periods and Semicolons

For most, periods are easy. They come at the end of sentences. Periods have other uses, such as at the end of some abbreviations, like *Mr., Dr.,* and *Capt.* Some agency abbreviations use periods, and some do not. One way to verify the use of periods in an agency abbreviation is to look up the agency online. You will see how they refer to themselves on their letterhead.

Semicolons can also be used in a sentence; in fact, they separate two complete sentences. Just remember not to capitalize the word following a semicolon unless it's a name requiring a capital letter. For example:

Officer Johnson raised the window; we entered the building.

One problem with semicolons is overuse. I suggest using no more than two to a page. Remember, semicolons join two sentences into one. You will have complete sentences already, so why not use a period? Look at the sentences below, and join them with a semicolon.

I told the teller to put the money in the bag. She complied.

John Smith called me about a burglary at his home. He has the serial numbers from the stolen guns.

I fingerprinted the refrigerator. I lifted four latent prints.

Commas

A theory some officers have about the use of commas is if you're not sure where they go, don't use any. Sentences that need commas and don't have them are difficult to understand. On the other hand, sentences that overuse commas create problems as well. Knowing a few simple comma rules can make things easier for you.

For a police report to be correct, we must cover the 4W+H in each event. In doing so, we will often connect words with other words and clauses. To do this, insert what is called a conjunction (a connector word) into a sentence. The English language uses seven conjunctions. They are *for, and, nor, but, or, yet,* and *so.* A way to remember them is by using the acronym FANBOYS:

F = for
A = and
N = nor
B = but
O = or
Y = yet
S = so

As you connect complete sentences, you should place a comma before the conjunction. That's why it's a connector. Just remember this connection must be between complete sentences (a complete thought with a subject and a verb).

Officer Jones arrested Dick Smith for DUI. He impounded Smith's car.

Here we have two sentences. *"Officer Jones arrested Dick Smith for DUI"* is the first sentence, and if that's all you wanted to say, you would end it with a period. *"He impounded Smith's car"* is the second sentence. You could also end that sentence with a period. However, to state what happened more efficiently, you can connect the two sentences with a conjunction.

Officer Jones arrested Dick Smith for DUI, and he impounded his car.

In the examples below, check and see if they are complete sentences. If they are, place a comma in the appropriate location.

The training was well intended but I could not read all of the materials.

I fired at the offender but missed him.

I interviewed Mary Smith about the domestic dispute and Detective Jerry Jones interviewed John Smith.

Officer Smith activated his blue lights and the driver pulled over to the curb.

Commas are also used to separate individual parts of an address. Note that there is no comma between the state and the ZIP code.

The suspect lived at 434 Green Street, Gainesville, GA 30571.

Commas are used in dates. Commas follow the day of the week, the numeral day of the month, and the year. Place a comma at the appropriate locations in this sentence:

On Monday October 1 2015 I responded to a robbery at 321 Main Street Lakewood Florida.

On Monday, October 1, 2015, I responded to a robbery at 321 Main Street, Lakewood, Florida.

We also use commas to join words in a series before the final conjunction in a sentence. Place a comma at the appropriate locations.

In the master bedroom, I collected a bloody towel a spent shell casing and a 9 mm Glock pistol.

In the master bedroom, I collected a bloody towel, a spent shell casing, and a 9 mm Glock pistol.

You will see that some agencies invert names: When providing names in reports, they use the last-name first. When this occurs, separate the last name from the first with a comma. No comma separates the first name and a middle name or initial.

Smith, Randy.
Jones, Robert A.
Jordan, Susan R.

As you can see, there are many uses for a comma. The examples I've used routinely occur in our reports.

Quotation Marks

During an interview with a witnesses, victim, or suspects, they will make statements or remarks you know you must emphasize in your report. To do so, you should include their exact words in your report and put quotation marks around it. A problem I've seen in many police reports is their overuse of quotation marks. Our reports are summaries of our activities; they are not transcripts. As you go about the business of including exact words of individuals in your report, do it sparingly. Save the quotes for the good stuff. Take a look at these sentences, and place quotation marks where needed.

> *At one point in the interview with James Jones, Jones became agitated and stated, I shot that SOB.*

> *At one point in the interview with James Jones, Jones became agitated and stated, "I shot that SOB."*

> *Arthur Sims admitted poisoning Mary Smith and stated, she deserved it.*

> *Arthur Sims admitted poisoning Mary Smith and stated, "She deserved it."*

In our reports, we frequently use quotation marks to illustrate someone's exact words or statement. We use commas to set off direct quotations. Look at this sentence and place the necessary commas and quotation marks.

> *A review of the officer Jones body worn camera system confirmed that just before the shooting he was heard yelling stop or I will shoot.*

> *A review of the officer Jones body worn camera system confirmed that just before the shooting, he was heard yelling, "Stop or I will shoot."*

Colons

A colon introduces an element of extra information that follows the sentence before the colon. It's used a lot in memorandum writing. We will discuss memorandum writing later on. For now, notice how the memorandum below uses a colon to format the introduction.

MEMORANDUM

To: Officer Jane Grant
From: Detective Harry Kurt
Date: May 23, 2016
Subject: Commendation

Apostrophe

Apostrophes show possession. In words illustrating possession, the apostrophe appears just before the letter "*s*". Look at the sentences below, and place an apostrophe at the correct locations.

Her attacker tore Marys clothing.

The detectives found a mens watch.

The fire started at Bob and Marys bar.

Here are the same sentences with correct apostrophe usage.

Her attacker tore Mary's clothing.

The detectives found a men's watch.

The fire started at Bob and Mary's bar.

Pronouns such as *ours, yours, hers,* and *theirs* have built in possession, so they don't need an apostrophe.

Contractions also use apostrophes. In contractions, we squeeze (contract) two words together by placing an apostrophe where letters have been left out. Here are some common words that are combined using an apostrophe.

I am: I'm

He is: He's

We have: We've

Will not: Won't

Could have: Could've

Look at the words below and combine them using an apostrophe.

Can not

Was not

Is not

Were not

They are

Parentheses

We often use parentheses in police reports to explain the meaning or add accuracy in a sentence.

During the search of the car, forty-five hundred dollars ($4500.00) was seized.

The Federal Bureau of Investigation (FBI) took over the bank robbery investigation.

The Florida Department of Law Enforcement (FDLE) was in charge of the case.

During the search of the crime scene, five (5) blood samples were recovered.

Capital Letters

Most people remember the rules about capital letters. We know that personal names, months of the year, and days of the week are capitalized, as well as cardinal directions (*North, South, West,* and *East).* Directions such as *northeast, southwest,* and *easterly* are not capitalized.

I had difficulty understanding John because he was from the South.

A double barrel shotgun was recovered in the southeast corner of the kitchen.

The names of streets, hospitals, and schools are also capitalized.

I attended Western Carolina University.

The assault victim was transported to St. Joseph Hospital.

The wreck occurred at the end of Main Street.

Words such as *Mother, Father, Aunt, General, Commissioner, Officer*, and *Mayor* should only be capitalized when used as part of a person's name.

At 2:00 p.m., I arrived at Mayor Weaver's office.

I directed Officer Hampton to transport Commissioner Roper to the hospital.

In this chapter, we reviewed some basic rules about sentence structure and punctuation that can help you write better reports. Most word processing software is equipped to aid you when you write. Of course, you can't rely totally on this software to proofread your reports and point out errors. Too many people get in the habit of relying on the "spell check" function, for example, which does not catch homophones (among other problems). We all tend to use the same words when we talk and write. Once you get in the habit of using and writing these words correctly, you will complete your reports with ease.

DISCUSSION TOPIC REVIEW

- Review the sample reports below describing events you have written about already. Look for the proper use of commas, semicolons, colons, quotation marks, capital letters, parentheses, and apostrophe usage.

Theft Report

On April 16 2016, at approximately 9:00 a.m., I (Officer Bill Smith) was dispatched to 421 Elm St. to take a theft report. I arrived at the address and spoke with the homeowner Jerry Jones. Mr. Jones stated that he lived at that address with his wife and two children. He and his family left for vacation on April 10 and came back home at about 8 o'clock that morning (April 16). When he got home, he noticed that his John Deere riding lawnmower that he stored under his deck was not there. The lawnmower is described as a John Deer, Model 31 with a 42-inch mowing deck and is green and yellow. I obtained the serial number for the lawnmower, which is 76514813, and Mr. Jones said it is valued at eight hundred dollars ($800.00).

Mr. Jones and I walked behind his house, and he showed me the area where the lawnmower had been kept. I was able to see tire tracks leading from the backyard and into a wooded area behind the home. I photographed the tire tracks.

No additional information was obtained from Jerry Jones.

ID data:
Jerry Jones
White male
DOB October 4, 1958
421 Elm Street, Clearlake, South Carolina 46120
Telephone number 803-555-7234

Burglary Report

On July 3, 2015, at approximately 7:00 p.m., I arrived at 421 Green Street to take a burglary report. I spoke with the homeowner Barry Griffin, who said he got home from work at about 6:00 p.m. He said he saw that his backdoor had been forced open. A flat screen television was missing from the living room. The master bedroom had been ransacked, and a 38-caliber revolver was missing. Mr. Griffin said he works at the trust Company Bank and goes to work at about 8:00 a.m. Mr. Griffin lives alone at that address.

I walked to the back door and saw the damage to the door and lock. I took photographs of this damage. Mr. Griffin showed me where his television had been mounted to the wall in the living room. I took pictures of the mounting bracket and the cables that had been cut. I looked in the master bedroom and saw that clothing had been taken from the dresser and the closet and thrown on the floor and bed. Mr. Griffin said his revolver was stored on a shelf in the closet. I took photographs of the bedroom.

Barry Griffin provided me with the serial number for the television. He said it was a Panasonic 42-inch television and was worth about $350.

He described his revolver as being a Smith & Wesson Model 60, serial number ABF7632 valued at about $325.

I provided an agency case number to Mr. Griffin and told him an investigator would contact him the next day.

ID data:
Barry Joseph Griffin
Black male
DOB: June 14, 1976
421 Green St., Tucson, AL 86751
Home phone: 423-555-8910
Employed Trust Company Bank, 22 Main St., Tucson, AL
Work phone: 423-555-2211

Neighborhood Canvass Report

On April 16, 2016, at approximately 10:00 a.m., I (Officer Bill Smith) conducted a neighborhood canvas in the vicinity of 421 Elm St. regarding the theft of a John Deere lawnmower from that location. I talked with Randy Taylor, who lives at 419 Elm Street, and Katie Hill, who lives at 420 Elm St. Mr. Taylor and Ms. Hill said that they did not see any suspicious activity at Jerry Jones' house during the time he and his family were on vacation.

I talked with Kevin Rose, who lives at 423 Elm St. and he said he remembered seeing a young boy in Jerry Jones' backyard pushing a lawnmower. He said he believed it was about 2:00 p.m. on April 12. He said the boy was a white male who appeared to be about sixteen years old. The boy was wearing blue jeans and a red sweatshirt. Mr. Rose said he thought the boy was cutting Jerry Jones' grass while they were on vacation, so he did not pay close attention. Mr. Ross stated he had not seen that boy in the neighborhood before.

ID data:
Kevin Rose
White male
DOB: June 6, 1987
423 Elm St., Clearlake, SC 47261

Answer Key

Theft Report

Missing comma after the date

On April 16, 2016, at approximately 9:00 a.m., I (Officer Bill Smith) was dispatched to 421 Elm St. to take a theft report. I arrived at the address and spoke with the homeowner Jerry Jones. Mr. Jones stated that he lived at that address with his wife and two children. He and his family left for vacation on April 10 and came back home at about 8 o'clock that morning (April 16). When he

Incorrect spelling of "Deere"

got home, he noticed that his John **Deere** riding lawnmower that he stored under his deck was not there. The lawnmower is described as a John Deere, Model 31 with a 42-inch mowing deck and is green and yellow. I obtained the serial number for the lawnmower, which is 76514813, and Mr. Jones said it is valued at eight hundred dollars ($800.00).

Mr. Jones and I walked behind his house, and he showed me the area where the lawnmower had been kept. I was able to see tire tracks leading from the backyard and into a wooded area behind the home. I photographed the tire tracks.

No additional information was obtained from Jerry Jones.

ID data:
Jerry Jones
White male
Missing colon DOB: October 4, 1958
421 Elm Street, Clearlake, South Carolina 46120
Missing colon Telephone number: 803-456-7234

Burglary Report

Missing comma after "homeowner"

On July 3, 2015, at approximately 7:00 p.m., I arrived at 421 Green Street to take a burglary report. I spoke with the homeowner, Barry Griffin, who said he got home from work at about 6:00 p.m. He said he saw that his backdoor had been forced open. A flat screen television was missing from the living room. The master bedroom had been ransacked, and a 38-caliber revolver was missing. Mr. Griffin said he works at the **Trust** Company Bank and goes to work at about 8:00 a.m. Mr. Griffin lives alone at that address.

Bank name should be capitalized

I walked to the back door and saw the damage to the door and lock. I took photographs of this damage. Mr. Griffin showed me where his television had been mounted to the wall in the living room. I took pictures of the mounting bracket and the cables that had been cut. I looked in the master bedroom and saw that clothing had been taken from the dresser and the closet and thrown on the floor and bed. Mr. Griffin said his revolver was stored on a shelf in the closet. I took photographs of the bedroom.

Barry Griffin provided me with the serial number for the television. He said it was a Panasonic 42-inch television and was worth about $350.

Failed to document the serial number of the TV.

He described his revolver as being a Smith & Wesson Model 60, serial number ABF7632 valued at about $325.

I provided an agency case number to Mr. Griffin and told him an investigator would contact him the next day.

ID data:
Barry Joseph Griffin
Black male
DOB: June 14, 1976
421 Green St., Tucson, AL 86751
Home phone: 423-678-8910

Missing colon

Employed: Trust Company Bank, 22 Main St., Tucson, AL
Work phone: 423-678-2211

Neighborhood Canvass Report

Incorrect spelling of "canvass"

On April 16, 2016, at approximately 10:00 a.m., I (Officer Bill Smith) conducted a neighborhood **canvass** in the vicinity of 421 Elm St. regarding the theft of a John Deere lawnmower from that location. I talked with Randy Taylor, who lives at 419 Elm Street, and Katie Hill, who lives at 420 Elm St. Mr. Taylor and Ms. Hill said that they did not see any suspicious activity at Jerry Jones' house during the time he and his family were on vacation.

Failed to provide a description of the boy

I talked with Kevin Rose, who lives at 423 Elm St., and he said he remembered seeing a young boy in Jerry Jones' backyard pushing a lawnmower. He said he believed it was about 2:00 p.m. on April 12. He said the boy was a white male who appeared to be about sixteen years old. The boy was wearing blue jeans and a red sweatshirt. Mr. Rose said he thought the boy was cutting Jerry Jones' grass while they were on vacation, so he did not pay close attention. Mr. Ross stated he had not seen that boy in the neighborhood before.

ID data:
Kevin Rose
White male
DOB: June 6, 1987
423 Elm St., Clearlake, SC 47261

Writing Reports That Contain More Action

CHAPTER 7

DISCUSSION TOPIC

The reports written so far have been short and simple. No evidence was seized, and no one was arrested. However, that is not always the case. Our reports often provide details of many different enforcement actions that become complicated and lengthy at times.

CHAPTER LEARNING OBJECTIVES

- Utilize sound note taking skills of events describing multiple actions.
- Demonstrate the ability to write reports of a more complicated nature.
- Analyze reports for errors.

I was in law enforcement for about thirty-six years and spent a good deal of that time writing and reviewing reports. I'm sure if I read some of my early ones, I would be embarrassed. But as time moves on, we all improve. I've designed this chapter to allow you to practice writing reports for actual law enforcement events. Each scenario contains an audio file, a transcript, and a sample report. Listen to the audio files of each scenario. Develop and practice good notetaking skills. Compare your notes to the transcript that follows each audio file and ensure accuracy. Organize your notes and prepare a narrative report about the event. Proofread your report for proper sentence structure, word usage, spelling, and punctuation.

Scenario 1: Shoplifting

In this exercise, you are called to Walmart regarding a shoplifting in progress. You talk with the loss prevention manager who gives you some basic information. You arrest the suspect as he leaves the store, and you recover some stolen DVDs. This is your first opportunity to handle evidence.

https://web.ung.edu/media/university-press/write-protect-serve-audio/shoplifting.m4a

Shoplifting Transcript

At 11:00 a.m. on December 2, 2015, you are dispatched to Walmart at 42 Industrial Blvd. regarding a shoplifting in progress. At 11:15 a.m., you arrive at Walmart and meet the Loss Prevention Supervisor, Janice Harper. Ms. Harper tells you that she has been watching a male shopper in the electronics department. She has seen the shopper place several DVDs inside his jacket. Harper says she is going to continue to watch the shopper, and if he leaves the store without paying for the DVDs, she will signal you. You go outside the Exit door and wait for Harper and the male shopper to come out. At about 11:30 a.m., you see the male shopper followed by Janice Harper walk out of the store. Harper signals you to approach the shopper. You stop the shopper as he is walking to a vehicle in the parking lot and identify him as Jeremy Thompson, white male, date of birth October 6, 1968. You ask him if he has any merchandise that he failed to pay for when leaving Walmart. He says, "No." You ask for and receive consent to search his jacket and recover six DVDs. At that time, Thompson admits to you that he had stolen the DVDs. You place him under arrest for shoplifting. The six DVDs are inventoried, photographed, and returned to Janice Harper. The value of the DVDs was determined to be $36. At about 12:00 p.m, you transport Thompson to the detention facility.

The identifying data for Jeremy Thompson is as follows:

Jeremy Dale Thompson
White male
DOB: October 6, 1968
491 Poplar St., Rome, Kentucky
Phone number: 768-555-2389

The identifying data for Janice Harper is as follows:

Janice Harper
White female
DOB: January 2, 1962
Loss Prevention Manager—Walmart
42 Industrial Blvd., Rome, Kentucky
Phone number: 768-555-8210

Shoplifting Report

At approximately 11:15 am, on December 2, 2015, I (Officer David Payne) responded to Walmart, at 42 Industrial Blvd. regarding a shoplifting in progress. I spoke with Janice Harper, the Loss Prevention Manager at Walmart, and learned that she had been watching a male shopper in the electronics department and had seen him conceal several DVDs inside his jacket. Ms. Harper said she was going to continue to watch the person, and if he left the store without paying for the DVDs, she would signal me.

I waited just outside the front Exit door, and at about 11:30 a.m., I saw Ms. Harper following the male shopper as he walked out of Walmart. This male, later identified as Jeremy Thompson, walked toward a vehicle in the parking lot. Before Thompson could enter his car, I approached him and asked if he had any merchandise that he had failed to pay for in Walmart. He responded by saying, "No." I asked for and received consent from Thompson to search him and found six DVDs concealed in a pocket in his jacket. At that time, he admitted he had not paid for the DVDs. I placed Thompson under arrest for shoplifting. The DVDs were inventoried, photographed, and returned to Janice Harper. The total value of the DVDs was $36. At about 12:00 p.m. I transported Jeremy Thompson to the detention facility.

ID data:
Jeremy Dale Thompson
White male
DOB: October 6, 1968
491 Poplar St., Rome, KY 76894
Telephone number: 768-555-2389

Janice Harper
White female
DOB: January 2, 1962
Loss Prevention Manager—Walmart
42 Industrial Blvd., Rome, Kentucky
Phone number: 768-555-8210

Scenario 2: Traffic Stop

Every few seconds in this nation, someone is pulled over while driving. A traffic stop is without a doubt the most dangerous event in law enforcement. In this scenario, you stop a car for a speeding violation. You arrest the driver for an outstanding warrant, impound the car, and issue a citation.

https://web.ung.edu/media/university-press/write-protect-serve-audio/traffic-stop.m4a

Traffic Stop Transcript

You are a patrol officer in your hometown police department. The date is April 30, 2016, and the time is 4:00 p.m. You're on routine patrol on Highway 369 monitoring traffic speeds using your in-car radar equipment. You meet a red Chevrolet pickup truck and clock its speed at 85 mph. The posted speed limit for that section of Highway 369 is 55 mph. As the pickup truck passes, you turn your patrol car around and pursue the truck. You catch up with the truck and activate your emergency lights and siren. The truck pulls over to the shoulder of the road.

You are able to determine that the tag number of the truck is HZR1657. You exit your patrol car and approach the driver side window of the truck. You see that one person occupies the truck. You inform the driver, identified as Jason Brown, the reason for your stop. You ask for and receive his license and insurance information.

Through dispatch, you check the status of Jason Brown's license and learn that it is valid. However, you learn that there is an active arrest warrant for Brown in your jurisdiction for a probation violation. You instruct Brown to get out of the truck and tell him that there is a warrant for his arrest. You conduct a pat-down search of Brown, handcuff him behind his back, double lock the handcuffs, and place him in the back seat of your patrol car.

You request dispatch send to your location the next list wrecker in order to impound Jason Brown's truck. Triple H wrecker service arrives at your location at about 5:00 p.m. You complete an agency impound report and provide a copy to Mark Johnson, the wrecker driver.

At about 5:30 p.m. you arrive at the Adult Detention Center and complete a traffic citation for speeding (85 mph in a 55 mph zone). Jason Brown is released to the staff at the detention center to be booked for the probation violation warrant.

ID data:
Jason Walter Brown
White male
DOB: October 2, 1976
894 Wood Circle, Cumming, GA 36781

Traffic Stop Report

On April 30, 2016, at approximately 4:00 p.m., I (Officer Jeremy Wright) was on routine patrol on Highway 369 in Cumming, Georgia. The speed limit posted on that section was 55 miles per hour. I clocked the speed of a red Chevrolet pickup truck traveling West on Highway 369 at 85 mph. I pursued the truck and activated my emergency lights and siren. The truck pulled over to the shoulder of the road and stopped. The tag number of the truck was HZR1657, and one person occupied it. I approached the driver, who was identified as Jason Brown, and told him the reason for the stop. He produced his license and insurance information and handed both documents to me. I checked the status of his license and learned that it was valid. I also learned from dispatch that there was an active arrest warrant for Mr. Brown for a probation violation. I told Mr. Brown to get out of his truck and placed him under arrest for the probation violation. I searched Mr. Brown, handcuff him behind his back (double locked the handcuffs), and placed him in the rear of my patrol car. I requested dispatch send the next list wrecker to my location. I completed an impound report and provided a copy of the report to Mark Johnson, the driver for Triple H wrecker service. At about 5:30 p.m., I arrived at the Adult Detention Center with Jason Brown and released him to the detention center staff to be processed for the probation violation warrant. I completed a traffic citation for speeding (85 mph in a 50 mph zone) and provided a copy to Brown.

ID data:
Jason Walter Brown
White male
DOB: October 2, 1976
894 Wood Circle, Cumming, GA 36781

Scenario 3: Domestic Dispute

Responding to a domestic dispute is challenging and dangerous. In this scenario, a patrol officer is the first to arrive at the scene and requests your assistance in the investigation. Details of the attack are given by the victim, and photographs are taken of her injuries. Her husband returns to the scene; he is then interviewed and arrested.

https://web.ung.edu/media/university-press/write-protect-serve-audio/domestic-dispute.m4a

Domestic Dispute Transcript

You are a detective in the Denver Colorado Police Department. The date is February 5, 2016, and the time is 10:00 a.m. You receive a telephone call from Patrol Officer Harry Morgan, who tells you that he has responded to 568 Mountainside Lane in Denver regarding a domestic dispute. He requests that you come to that address and assist him with the investigation.

You arrive at 568 Mountainside Lane at 10:30 a.m. and meet with Officer Morgan. He tells you that he was dispatched to that address following a 911 call that was placed by Jennifer Logan. Ms. Logan lives at that address. When he arrived, he talked with Ms. Logan and learned that her husband Jeff Logan, who also lives there, had beaten her up. You see bruises on the neck of Ms. Logan and scratches on her face. She tells you she and her husband, Jeff, have been arguing for the past two weeks and were making plans to get a divorce. She says that on the previous evening (February 4, 2016), she and her husband were talking about dividing their property following the divorce. She stated they got into an argument, and her husband began to drink heavily. Jeff Logan was drinking from a bottle of Ancient Age bourbon. She said at one point her husband grabbed her around her neck and began to choke her. She was able to escape, but he again grabbed her and hit her in the face causing scratches. Jeff Logan left in his 2009 Chevrolet Cruz.

Officer Morgan called EMS to treat the injuries of Jennifer Logan. You photograph the injuries to her neck and face. You also see a half-empty quart bottle of Ancient Age bourbon on the kitchen counter and photograph it.

As EMS is leaving the house, Jeff Logan returns. You meet with Logan on the front porch and detect a strong odor of alcohol. He confirms to you that he and his wife had been arguing about their upcoming divorce and were having trouble deciding how to divide their property. He said he had a few drinks and got into a physical fight with his wife. Jeff Logan said that he must've had too much to drink, and he was sorry.

Due to the injuries to Jennifer Logan, you arrest Jeff Logan, charging him with violation of the Family Violence Law. Officer Morgan administers a field Breathalyzer exam to Jeff Logan, which indicated his blood-alcohol level was .15%. Officer Morgan charges Jeff Logan with driving under the influence. Officer Harry Morgan transports Logan to the Denver City Jail.

ID data:
Jeffrey Wayne Logan
White male
DOB: July 4, 1982
568 Mountainside Lane, Denver, CO 73289
Telephone number: 678-555-5059

Jennifer René Logan
White female
DOB: May 8, 1986
568 Mountainside Lane, Denver, CO 73289
Telephone number: 678-555-5059

Domestic Dispute Report

On February 5, 2016, at about 10:00 a.m., I (Detective Marty James) received a telephone call from Officer Harry Morgan who told me he had responded to a domestic dispute at 568 Mountainside Lane in Denver. He requested I meet him at that address to assist in the investigation.

At about 10:30 a.m, I arrived at 568 Mountainside Lane and met with Officer Morgan. He told me that Jennifer Logan, who lives at that address, placed a 911 call. He stated that when he met with Ms. Logan, he observed bruises on her neck and scratches on her face. Ms. Logan said that she and her husband, Jeff Logan, were in the process of getting a divorce and had been arguing about the division of their personal property. She said that on the evening of February 4, 2016, her husband was drinking heavily, and they began to argue. She said that her husband grabbed her by the neck and began to choke her and hit her in the face, causing scratches. Jeff Logan then left the house driving a 2009 Chevrolet Cruz.

Officer Morgan called EMS to treat the injuries of Jennifer Logan, and I took photographs of her neck and face. I saw a bottle of Ancient Age Bourbon on the kitchen counter and took photographs of it.

As I was talking with Jennifer Logan, Jeff Logan arrived at the house driving the Chevrolet Cruz. I talked with Jeff Logan on the front porch and detected a strong odor of alcohol. He told me that the previous evening, he and his wife had been arguing about their upcoming divorce, and he must have had too much to drink. Jeff Logan said he was sorry.

Due to the visible injuries to Jennifer Logan, I placed Jeff Logan under arrest for violation of the Family Violence Law. Officer Morgan administered a field Breathalyzer exam to Jeff Logan, which measured .15%. Officer Morgan charged Jeff Logan with driving under the influence and transported him to the Denver City Jail.

ID data:
Jeffrey Wayne Logan
White male
DOB: July 4, 1982
568 Mountainside Ln., Denver, CO 73289
Telephone number: 678-555-5059

Jennifer René Logan
White female
DOB: May 8, 1986
568 Mountainside Ln., Denver, CO 73289
Telephone number: 678-555-5059

Scenario 4: Murder Interview

In this event, you arrive at a house where a murder has occurred. You speak with a deputy sheriff who gives you details about the scene. There are two victims shot. One is dead at the scene, and the other one died on the way to the hospital.

https://web.ung.edu/media/university-press/write-protect-serve-audio/murder-interview.m4a

Murder Interview Transcript

You are a Special Agent with the Georgia Bureau of Investigation. The date is February 9, 2011, and the time is 5:00 a.m. You have been asked to respond to a death investigation in Pickens

County, Georgia. At about 5:30 a.m., you arrive at 293 Stone Road and speak with Chris Jones, an EMS/Fire employee. You see two other officers at the scene and identified them as April Young and Greg Joseph. Chris Jones says that he was dispatched to the scene following a 911 call. When he got to the house, he entered through the front door and smelled what he believed to be gunpowder. He said he walked through the house and saw in a bedroom a man and a woman lying on the floor. Both had been shot. He said he examined the woman and determined she was dead. The man was alive and was carried from the house on a stretcher to the ambulance. The man asked Jones to call his daughter. Chris Jones stated the man died on the way to the hospital.

ID data:
Chris Jones
Black male
DOB: January 5, 1965
Employed: Pickens County EMS/Fire service
421 Camp Road, Jasper, GA 30143
Telephone number: 706-555-9111

Murder Interview Report

On February 9, 2011, at approximately 5:00 a.m., I, Special Agent Jennifer Wright of the Georgia Bureau of Investigation (GBI), responded to a death investigation in Pickens County, Georgia. I arrived at 293 Stone Rd. at about 5:30 a.m. and spoke with Chris Jones, an EMS/Fire employee. I also saw at the scene two police officers who I identified as April Young and Greg Joseph. Chris Jones told me he was dispatched to that address following a 911 call. When he arrived, he entered through the front door and smelled what he believed to be gunpowder in the air. In a bedroom of the house, he located a man and a woman who had been shot. He examined the woman and determined she was dead. The man was placed on a stretcher and carried from the house to the ambulance, during which time he asked Jones to call his daughter. The man died on the way to the hospital.

ID data:
Chris Jones
Black male
DOB: January 5, 1965
Employed: Pickens County EMS/Fire service
421 Camp Road, Jasper, GA 30143
Telephone number: 706-555-9111

Scenario 5: Murder Crime Scene

Following the interview with the deputy sheriff in Scenario 4, you begin to process the crime scene. You describe in detail the area outside the house, including several cars. You make entry to the house through the carport door, and you examine each room. You find the female victim in the master bedroom. She is dead of multiple gunshot wounds. You describe the scene and collect evidence.

Murder Crime Scene Transcript
You are a Special Agent with the Georgia Bureau of Investigation and trained as a crime scene specialist. The date is February 9, 2011; the time is 7:15 a.m. You arrive at 293 Stone Rd. and see the scene secured with yellow crime scene tape. You meet with Deputy Sheriff Ray Chandler and learn that two victims in the investigation suffered gunshot wounds. The male victim is Steve Campbell. The female victim is Sherry Campbell. He tells you that each victim was shot twice and that Steve Campbell was taken from the scene and died on the way to the hospital. Sherry Campbell was dead in the master bedroom. Chandler tells you EMS personnel entered through the front door and placed Steve Campbell on a stretcher. There are drops of blood in the hallway of the residence leading out the front door and continuing to the front yard. This

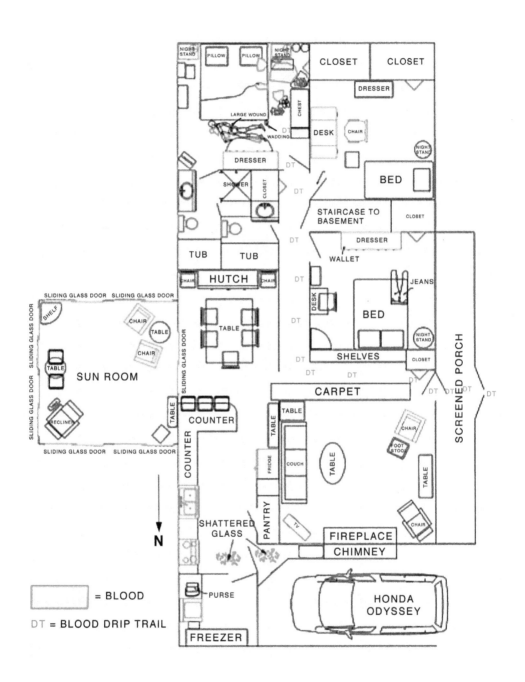

blood trail was created as Steve Campbell was bleeding while he was carried to the ambulance.

The sky is clear, and the temperature is 28°F. You use your Canon Rebel digital camera to photograph the scene in its entirety. These photographs will be transferred to a DVD later and stored in the rear of the case file. A sketch is completed of the scene, including measurements. The house is a wood frame, single-family dwelling with brown wood siding and a shingled roof. It has a partially finished basement. The front door of the house opens to the west, and a screened in porch with double doors is on the west side of the house. An above ground swimming pool with a wooden deck is to the northeast of the house. A wood frame barn is to the southwest of the house. An older model white and gray Chevrolet pickup truck, tag number ALK 0262, is in the driveway. It appears to be inoperable. A blue Ford tractor and a blue Chevrolet Cavalier with Georgia tag 388 AXP are parked near the barn. A red Ford Ranger pickup truck with Georgia tag 4672SB is in the front yard. A white Honda Odyssey minivan with Georgia tag 415BRD is in the carport. You search these vehicles and the barn and do not find any evidence.

In the carport, there is a door leading into the kitchen. The door contains nine separate panes of glass. The lower right-hand corner pane of glass closest to the lock is shattered.

There is a laundry room located in the northwest corner directly north of the kitchen. A black purse containing the identification of Sherry Campbell is on the top of the dryer.

A dining room is south of the kitchen. You search the dining room and find no evidence. A sunroom is located east of the dining room with the exterior doors closed but unlocked. You search this room and find no evidence.

The living room is to the south of the carport. There is no evidence recovered in the living room.

There are two bedrooms located on the west side of the hallway traveling to the south end of the house. In the first bedroom, you see a pair of men's blue jeans on the bed and a wallet containing the identification of Steve Campbell on the dresser. A bathroom is in the hallway; there was no evidence located in the bathroom. Another bedroom is on the southwest corner of the house. You search this bedroom and find no evidence.

The master bedroom is on the southeast corner of the house. A drip trail of blood extends from the southwest corner of this bedroom, out of the bedroom, and down the hallway. You see an orange Old Navy extra-large shirt containing blood spatter stains hanging from one of the handles on the chest. There is a pair of men's blue jeans and a pair of dark colored men's slippers on the floor each containing blood spatter stains. There are blood transfer stains on top of the nightstand. There is a large pool of blood on the bed near a pillow. One of the bedposts appears to have been shot, and you see wood splinters throughout the bedroom. On the bed, there are numerous BBs from a shotgun shell. You collect 29 BBs from on the bed and floor as well as one plastic shotgun wadding. These were seized and appear on property receipt E532690.

The body of Sherry Campbell is lying on the floor just north of the bed. She has red hair and is wearing light-colored pajama type pants and a white nightshirt. Her right arm is extended, and you see an open wound just above her right wrist exposing broken bones. There is a large open wound on the left side of her torso. There are blood transfer stains and blood spatter stains on her face. At about 11:53 a.m., the body of Sherry Campbell was placed in a dark-colored disaster bag and removed from the scene by Kevin Roper, the Pickens County coroner.

At 12:30 p.m., you finish processing the scene and leave.

Murder Crime Scene Report

On February 9, 2011, at 7:15 a.m., I (place name here) arrived at 293 Stone Rd., Jasper, GA. The scene was secured with yellow crime scene tape. The sky was clear, and the temperature was 28°F. Deputy Sheriff Ray Chandler was already at the scene and informed me of the situation. He said that there were two victims, both of whom had been shot in the home. Deputy Chandler said the male victim was Steve Campbell and that he was still alive when EMS employees arrived. Members of EMS entered the home through the front door, placed Steve Campbell on a stretcher, and carried him from the master bedroom to an ambulance parked outside. Steve Campbell was bleeding from his wounds, and a drip trail of blood could be seen leading from the master bedroom, out the front door, and onto the sidewalk. Steve Campbell died on the way to the hospital. The second victim was a female named Sherry Campbell. Ms. Campbell had been shot twice and was dead in the master bedroom.

The house at 293 Stone Rd. was a wood frame, single-family home with brown wood siding and a shingled roof. It also has a partially finished basement. On the west side of the home, there was a screened-in porch, and to the northwest of the home, there was an above ground swimming pool. There was a barn to the southwest of the home. A blue Ford tractor and a Chevrolet Cavalier, bearing tag number 388A XP, was near the barn. A red Ford Ranger pickup truck, bearing tag number 4672SB, was in the front yard. In the carport, there was a white Odyssey minivan, bearing tag number 415BRD. The barn and all the vehicles were searched; no evidence was found.

The carport door had nine panes of glass in the top half of the door. The pane closest to the lock was shattered. The carport door entered into the kitchen, and there was a laundry room to the north. On top of the dryer in the laundry room, there was a black purse containing the identification of Sherry Campbell. No other evidence was found in the laundry room. The kitchen and dining room was searched, and no evidence was found. There was a sunroom east of the dining room with both doors closed but unlocked. No evidence was found in the sunroom. There were two bedrooms on the west side of the hallway leading to the south end of the house. In the first bedroom, there was a pair of men's blue jeans on the bed and a wallet containing the identification of Steve Campbell on the dresser. The second bedroom contained no evidence. There was a bathroom in the hallway, and it contained no evidence. In the southeast corner of the home was the master bedroom. There was a blood drip trail leading from the southwest corner of the master bedroom, down the hallway, and out the front door. Hanging from the dresser in the master bedroom was an orange Old Navy shirt that contained blood spatter stains. A pair of men's blue jeans and a pair of dark colored men's slippers were on the master bedroom floor, and each contains bloodstains. There was a pool of blood on the bed near a pillow. It appeared a bedpost had been shot, and wood splinters were on the bed and floor. Twenty-nine (29) BBs and one (1) shotgun wadding were recovered in the master bed-room. They were seized and appear on property receipt E532690. The body of Sherry Campbell was lying on the floor just north of the bed. She was wearing light-colored pajama pants and a white nightshirt. Ms. Campbell's right arm was extended, and there was an open wound above her right wrist that exposed broken bones. She also had an open wound on the left side of her torso. There was blood transfer and blood spatter stains on Ms. Campbell's face.

At about 11:53 a.m., the body of Sherry Campbell was placed in a dark-colored disaster bag and taken from the scene by Kevin Roper, the Pickens County coroner. At about 12:30 p.m., I finished processing the scene and left.

The scene was photographed in its entirety using a Canon Rebel digital camera. The photographs will be downloaded to a DVD and stored in the rear of the case file. A sketch of the entire scene, as well as measurements, will be attached to this report.

Scenario 6: Undercover Drug Buy

Officers assigned to drug units frequently work undercover. They develop informants and identify suspects. One of the most effective investigative techniques in a drug investigation is to obtain a hand-to-hand drug buy from a drug dealer. In this event, you are introduced to Larry Jones, a local drug dealer, and arrange to meet him to make the buy. Surveillance cameras are activated on yourself and the CI. You buy the methamphetamine, seal it in an evidence bag, and store it in the secure evidence room.

https://web.ung.edu/media/university-press/write-protect-serve-audio/drug-buy.m4a

Evidence photo of illegal drugs recovered by law enforcement.

Undercover Drug Buy Transcript

It is approximately 6:00 p.m. on October 15, 2015. You receive a telephone call from a confidential informant, coded by your agency as CI 13. The source tells you that Larry Jones contacted him earlier in the day. Jones asked the CI if he needed to buy methamphetamine. The CI told Jones that he did not have any money at that time but had a friend that did. Larry Jones agreed to sell methamphetamine to CI 13's friend.

At about 6:30 p.m., you and your partner, Detective Ralph Smith, meet CI 13. You prepare CI 13 to take you to meet with Larry Jones. Detective Smith searches the CI and his car. No contraband/drugs are found. An audio/video camera is concealed in the clothing of the CI. A camera is also concealed in your clothing. You are in possession of $1500, which had previously been photocopied. The recorders are activated, and Detective Smith follows you and the CI to the residence of Larry Jones. He stops in an area allowing him to see the house. At about 7:30 p.m., you and the CI enter the house through the front door, and you are introduced to Larry Jones. You tell Jones you want to buy one ounce of methamphetamine. Jones walked into another room in the house and returned to the living room with a plastic bag containing a crystalline substance. He hands the bag to you, and you pay him $1500. At about 7:45 p.m., you and the CI leave.

At 8:00 PM, you and the CI meet with Detective Smith. Smith searches the CI and his vehicle again and does not locate any contraband/drugs. You retrieve the audio/video recorder from the CI and deactivate it and yours.

You seal the bag of methamphetamine in a plastic evidence bag and place your initials and the date on the bag. The bag of methamphetamine is described on evidence receipt number B73674 and locked in the secure evidence room by you that night.

Undercover Drug Buy Report

On October 15, 2015 at approximately 6:00 p.m., I (place name here) received a telephone call from CI 13. The source told me that he talked with Larry Jones at about 5:30 p.m., and that Jones asked him if he needed to buy any methamphetamine. CI 13 said that he did not have any money, but a friend of his did. The source stated Larry Jones said it would be okay to bring the friend.

At about 6:30 p.m., my partner, Detective Ralph Smith, and I met with CI 13 and made plans for me to buy the methamphetamine from Jones. As per policy, Detective Smith searched the person and vehicle of CI 13 and found no contraband. An audio/video camera was concealed in the clothing of the CI as well as in my clothing. I was in possession of $1500.00 of official agency funds to use to purchase the methamphetamine. The money previously had been photocopied.

I activated the recording devices, and Detective Smith followed us to the residence of Larry Jones and took a position allowing him to see the house. At approximately 7:30 p.m., I entered through the front door and was introduced to Larry Jones by the CI. I told Jones I wanted to purchase one ounce of methamphetamine. Jones walked into another room of the house and returned to the living room with a plastic bag containing a crystalline substance. I paid Jones the $1500.00, and he handed me the bag of methamphetamine. At about 7:45 p.m., we left.

At about 8:00 p.m., we met with Detective Smith at a predetermined location. Detective Smith searched the person and car of the CI and found no contraband. I retrieved and deactivated the recording devices. The bag of suspected methamphetamine was sealed in a plastic evidence bag, and I placed my initials and the date on the bag. The evidence was described on property receipt B73674 and secured by me in the evidence locker later that night.

Scenario 7: Execution of Search Warrant Following Drug Buy

In this scenario, you are joined by several other detectives and execute a search warrant. This event builds on the information developed in Scenario 6. During the search, several pieces of evidence are found in different areas of the house. The evidence is collected, and property receipts are completed. Larry Jones is arrested. During the search, the girlfriend of Jones arrives at the house. She consents to a search, and more drugs are located in her purse. She is arrested.

https://web.ung.edu/media/university-press/write-protect-serve-audio/execution-search-warrant.m4a

Execution of Search Warrant Transcript

You have decided to execute a search warrant at the residence of Larry Jones. Your raid team consists of the following detectives: Ralph Smith, Greg Harvey, Steve Duncan, Mike Denson, Randall Jones, and Jennifer Wright.

At approximately 6:00 p.m. on October 20, 2015, you arrive at the residence of Larry Jones at 421 Decatur Rd., Atlanta, Georgia. You make entry through the front door and find Larry Jones standing in the living room. He was handcuffed and seated on the couch. The search of the residence begins at about 6:15 p.m.

Detective Ralph Smith locates, under the bed in the master bedroom, a set of digital scales. Next to the scales, he finds a box of quart-sized plastic sandwich bags. He describes these items on property receipt number A4670.

Detective Mike Denson searches the kitchen. In the refrigerator, he finds a gallon-sized plastic bag containing what he believed to be methamphetamine. He seizes the bag and describes it on property receipt number A6734.

Detective Steve Duncan searches the bathroom and finds a metal box in a cabinet containing money. He counts the money and determines that it is $15,421. Detective Mike Denson verifies the count. The money is seized and sealed in a plastic evidence bag and described on property receipt number C7489.

Detective Jennifer Wright searches Larry Jones and finds in his right front pocket a cell phone. It is seized and sealed in a plastic evidence bag and described on property receipt number Z8970.

At about 7:00 PM a female, later identified as Mary Smith, arrived at the house. You talked with Smith and learned that she lived with Larry Jones and had been staying there for about a month. You asked for and obtained consent from Smith to search her car and her purse. Detective Randall Jones located in her purse a small plastic bag containing what appeared to be methamphetamine. Also in the purse, he found $8,000.00. The count is verified by Detective Denson, and the money is sealed in evidence bag J4380. The bag of suspected methamphetamine was sealed in evidence bag J4379. Nothing of evidentiary value was found in Smith's car. Mary Smith was arrested, handcuffed, and seated on the couch in the living room next to Larry Jones.

At about 8:30 p.m., the search was concluded. Larry Jones was provided with an inventory of items that were seized and a copy of the search warrant. He and Mary Smith were transported to the detention facility by patrol officer Kevin Larson.

The residence of Larry Jones was secured at about 8:30 p.m. and all officers left the scene.

ID data:
Larry Stephen Jones
White male
DOB: October 20, 1972
6'3" tall, 280 pounds
421 Decatur Rd., Atlanta, GA 30674
Cell phone number: 706-555-1032

Mary Elaine Smith
White female
DOB: February 6, 1979
5'1" tall, 93 pounds
421 Decatur Rd., Atlanta, GA 30674
Cell phone number: 706-555-5432

Execution of Search Warrant Report

On October 20, 2015, I (your name here) assembled a raid team for the purpose of executing a search warrant at the residence of Larry Jones. The raid team consisted of Detectives Ralph Smith, Greg Harvey, Steve Duncan, Mike Denson, Randall Jones, and Jennifer Wright.

At approximately 6:00 p.m., we arrived at the residence of Larry Jones, at 421 Decatur Rd., Atlanta, GA. We made entry through the front door and found Larry Jones standing in the living room. He was handcuffed and seated on the couch. The search of the residence began at about 6:15 p.m.

Detective Ralph Smith, while searching the master bedroom, found a set of digital scales under the bed. Next to the scales, he found a box of quart-sized plastic sandwich bags. He described these items on property receipt A4670.

Detective Mike Denson searched the kitchen and found in the refrigerator a gallon-sized plastic bag containing what he believed to be methamphetamine. He placed the plastic bag into an evidence bag, placed his initials and the date on the bag, and described it on property receipt number A6734.

Detective Steve Duncan found a metal box containing United States currency in a cabinet in the bathroom. He counted the money and determined that it was $15,421.00. Detective Denson verified the count. The money was seized and sealed in a plastic evidence bag and described on property receipt number C7489.

Detective Jennifer Wright searched Larry Jones and found in his right front pocket a cell phone. She seized the phone, sealed it in a plastic evidence bag, and described it on property receipt number Z8970.

At about 7:00 p.m, a female arrived at the house. She was identified as Mary Smith, the girlfriend of Larry Jones. I asked for and obtained consent from her to search her car and her purse. Detective Ralph Jones found in her purse a small plastic bag containing what appeared to be methamphetamine. He found $8000.00 in U.S. currency in the purse. Detective Denson verified the count, and the money was sealed in an evidence bag and described on property receipt number J4380. Nothing of evidentiary value was found in her car. Detective Jones placed the bag of suspected methamphetamine in an evidence bag, placed his initials and date on the bag, and described it on property receipt number J4379.

At about 8:30 p.m., the search was concluded. I provided Larry Jones with a copy of the search warrant and an inventory of the items that were seized. He and Mary Smith were transported to the detention facility by Patrol Officer Kevin Larson.

The residence of Larry Jones was secured at about 8:30 p.m. and all officers left the scene.

ID data:
Larry Stephen Jones
White male
DOB: October 20, 1972
6'3" tall, 280 pounds
421 Decatur Rd., Atlanta, GA 30674
Cell phone number: 706-555-1032

Mary Elaine Smith
White female
DOB: February 6, 1979
5'1" tall, 93 pounds
421 Decatur Rd., Atlanta, GA 30674
Cell phone number: 706-555-5434

DISCUSSION TOPIC REVIEW

By now in your report-writing progression, you have developed great notetaking skills, developed formatting choices you prefer, and have completed reports describing a wide array of situations. You have proofread, found mistakes, and edited your reports. All it takes now is practice, which you will most certainly get.

Compliance Writing

CHAPTER 8

DISCUSSION TOPIC

Modern agencies are constantly striving to be more professional and effective. The ability to implement policies and procedures and prove compliance with them is becoming the norm.

According to the Fourth Amendment of the U.S. Constitution:

The right of the people to be secure in their persons, houses, papers, and effects, against unreasonable searches and seizures, shall not be violated, and no Warrants shall issue, but upon probable cause, supported by Oath or affirmation, and particularly describing the place to be searched, and the persons or things to be seized.

The ability to collect and document detailed information and assimilate it in a document that meets the legal standards, as outlined in the Constitution, is critical.

Through electronic messaging, a new language has emerged as people are now writing things like LOL, TBT, and OMG. Using those acronyms is fine when communicating informally. However, there are times when a more formal method of communication is required. This communication often takes the form of a memorandum.

A witness is sworn in by a judge.

CHAPTER LEARNING OBJECTIVES

Accreditation

- Identify the agencies that have developed and implemented accreditation and certification standards.
- Describe examples of the goals of accreditation and certification.
- Demonstrate the ability to apply report writing to compliance requirements.

Search and Seizure

- Understand the Fourth Amendment and its application to events encountered by law enforcement officers.
- Develop a clear understanding of the most common exceptions to the warrant requirement.
- Learn the definition of probable cause.
- Demonstrate the ability to collect information and draft a search warrant affidavit that meets current legal standards.

Memorandum Writing

- Understand the many purposes of a memorandum.
- Recognize standard memorandum formatting.
- Develop a clear understanding of the different sections contained in the body of a memorandum.

As discussed previously, you will encounter many types of events in law enforcement. You will write external reports that describe circumstances and facts learned about criminal activity and some that do not. Reports describing lost/found property, no-fault automobile accidents, animal control issues, and wellness checks are examples of reports that do not involve criminal activity. Internal reports can include use of force reports, training requests, leave requests, transfer requests, commendations, and disciplinary action, to name a few. Routinely detectives combine information contained in both criminal and noncriminal reports during their investigations in order to obtain search warrants. Detectives present this document, called an "affidavit," to a judicial officer in support of a request to search someone, something, or somewhere. Search warrant affidavits are one of the most scrutinized documents in the criminal justice system.

Accreditation/Certification

Early in my career, I was talking to the sheriff of a small North Georgia county. I was assigned to assist his investigator when a serious crime occurred. One day, I was in the Sheriff's office and asked him what his policy was for handling a certain issue involved in that investigation. He responded by saying his department had no policies at all. When asked why, he said that a neighboring sheriff had a lot of policies and procedures and was sued for occasionally not following them. Therefore, this sheriff thought it was better not to have policies anyone in his department could violate so as to prevent civil action. Of course, his department was lacking in many ways compared to modern-day departments. However, as time passed and a new sheriff was elected, things began to change. No longer could this agency and others like it fight progress. The new sheriff was able to get a copy of the policy manual from the neighboring county and eventually adopted modern-day policies and procedures.

In 1979, the Commission on Accreditation for Law Enforcement Agencies, Inc. (CALEA) was created. It was an effort by the International Association of Chiefs of Police, the National Organization of Black Law Enforcement Executives (NOBLE), the National Sheriff's Association (NSA), and the Police Executive Research Forum (PERF). These groups established several goals:

- Strengthen crime prevention and control capabilities
- Formalize essential management procedures
- Establish fair and nondiscriminatory personnel practices
- Improve service delivery
- Solidify interagency cooperation and coordination
- Increase community and staff confidence in the agency

It required agencies to develop a uniform set of written directives that they must follow in their departments. These directives addressed many aspects of day-to-day operations of a law enforcement agency. Everything from training standards to handcuffing became part of the directives manual. CALEA accreditation became the gold standard for agencies to strive to attain.

Some states began to develop their certification programs using CALEA as a model. In Georgia, the Georgia Association of Chiefs of Police (GACP) manages the state certification process. It developed standards of operation and a system to certify law enforcement agencies who comply with those criteria. It also developed a recertification program whereby agencies must prove that they are in fact following the established directives.

National accreditation and state certification definitely have improved law enforcement agencies. Here are a few examples of accreditation standards:

- Following the arrest of a suspect and before their transportation to a detention facility, the suspect will be searched and handcuffed behind their back. The handcuffs will be double locked.
- An inventory search of all vehicles will be completed if the vehicle is being impounded.
- Miranda rights will be read to all suspects before being questioned.
- Employees must maintain and care for all issued equipment.
- Employees must complete a legal update training course annually.

National accreditation requires compliance with several hundred standards. Some state certifications have between one hundred and two hundred standards. Periodically, agencies will be examined to ensure they are in compliance.

How does all this pertain to report writing? The best method to prove compliance with most of the established standards is to produce a report that outlines the performance of certain required activities. For instance, a report of an interview with the suspect during which they were advised of their Miranda rights before questioning would be proof that the standard was followed. Similarly, a report outlining an inventory search of a vehicle before it was impounded would be proof of that standard being followed. If your agency is accredited or certified, you should expect that your reports will be reviewed to ensure your actions in the field meet all the standards.

Search and Seizure

As I prepared to write this book, I talked with several leaders in the law enforcement community who believe firmly that report writing needs to be improved. Most said they would like to see more instruction as it relates to writing one of the most critical documents in police work: a search warrant affidavit.

To put it plainly, the Fourth Amendment was written to protect citizens from the government. The other amendments do as well. Those of us in law enforcement and other areas of the criminal justice system are expected to have a working knowledge of our guaranteed constitutional rights and how to apply these rights in our work. For instance, we must possess the ability to recognize when the search of a person, place, or thing is subject to the Fourth Amendment and when the search is not. We therefore must be familiar with many of the laws that address search and seizure. The majority of the case law addresses one critical aspect known as "an expectation of privacy." In other words, does a person have an expectation of privacy in the area to be searched? If based on your knowledge, training, and the circumstances, you determine that there is no expectation of privacy by an individual, then no search warrant is needed. For instance, one case dealt with an investigative technique called a "Trash Pull." The court determined that if an individual moves their garbage cans to the curb in front of their home to await garbage pickup, they no longer have an expectation of privacy of the trash can's contents. Consequently, in the middle of the night, investigators were able to remove the trash from the can and search it for evidence without a warrant.

Another important factor to be familiar with is something called the "Plain View Doctrine." This rule allows law enforcement, who are in their "legal shoes" during a citizen/police encounter, to legally seize evidence in plain view without a warrant. An example of such legal seizure might occur during a legitimate investigation of a burglary in a neighborhood. Officers routinely conduct a neighborhood canvass to find out if any of the neighbors had any information about the burglary. One officer walks up to the front porch of a neighbor's home and sees a marijuana plant growing in a bucket. The officer is certainly in their legal shoes as they conduct a neighborhood canvass. Therefore, the officer can seize the marijuana plant without first having to obtain a search warrant. Of course, many other occasions happen when the Plain View Doctrine would apply.

The courts have also allowed law enforcement to search someone's clothing following a lawful arrest, even if law enforcement doesn't have a search warrant. This rule is called "Search Incident to Arrest." The important thing to remember about this rule is the arrest must be lawful.

From time to time, police officers will ask individuals for their permission to search them, their homes, or place of business. For a "Consent Search" to be lawful, consent must be given freely and voluntarily without the promise of any reward or sanction. In other words, officers cannot for instance, promise someone that no arrest would be made if consent to search a location were given.

That brings us to the occasions when no consent to search is given, the Plain View Doctrine is not in play, and we have determined that certain individuals do in fact have an expectation of privacy, as contemplated by the Constitution. When you read the Fourth Amendment, you will see two famous words: *probable cause*. As we go about our daily duty, we base a good deal of our actions on probable cause. The definition of probable cause, as discussed in Black's Law Dictionary, is as follows:

Probable cause to search for evidence or to seize evidence requires that an officer is possessed of sufficient facts and circumstances as would lead a reasonable person to believe that evidence or contraband relating to criminal activity will be found in the location to be searched.

Every day in almost every police agency, officers are working to establish probable cause to search for evidence of criminal activity. Without getting too entangled in the weeds of the hundreds of court decisions that address search and seizure, let us review some key factors.

In order to apply for a search warrant, officers are required to document (write down) what they believe to be sufficient probable cause to conduct a search. They then present the information to a neutral magistrate who will make a determination whether or not probable cause exists. The officer must provide the magistrate with a substantial basis—not merely their conclusions—for determining probable cause.

Four stages will occur when officers are working to obtain a search warrant. First, officers prepare an affidavit, which sets out certain information to be considered by the magistrate. Second, there is a separate document that the magistrate will sign if the warrant is issued. This document authorizes the search to be conducted and is frequently referred to as the search warrant order. Third, the officers carry out the search and provide a copy of the search warrant order to the suspect or leave it in a prominent place where the search occurred. Fourth, the officer must appear before the magistrate following the search and notify them when the search was conducted, what (if any) evidence was seized, and the name of the person who received a copy of the warrant order or the location where it was left at the scene.

Preparing a search warrant affidavit is not difficult so long as you remember the legal requirements. Sworn officers are the only ones who can apply for a search warrant. The officer prepares the affidavit in sections. The first section is an introductory statement which confirms to the magistrate that you are a sworn police officer in good standing. It also lists the name of your agency and how long you have worked there. Some officers also include any training they have that would be relevant for the magistrate to consider.

The second section contains a specific description of where the search will take place. If you will be searching a house, you must include the address and a good description of it. Here is an example: "434 Green St., Houston, TX, a single-family brick house with a front porch and a two-car garage, with a mailbox at the entrance to a concrete driveway displaying the numbers 434." If you were searching a car, a complete description of the car, including the tag number and VIN, would fulfill these requirements. This is necessary because the courts have said officers must state specifically where or what they are going to search.

The next section is a description of the evidence that you believe will be found. It too must be specific. For instance, if you are looking for a weapon used in a murder, you must describe as best you can what it is and what it looks like. It is insufficient to search for "fruits of the crime of murder." You must be specific. The same is true if you were searching for cocaine, methamphetamine, or marijuana. It would be insufficient to say "drug evidence." Another legal requirement relates to searches. In several court decisions, you will encounter the phrase, "scope of the search." This phrase means that whatever you're looking for can be found where you're looking. For instance, if you're looking for a 357-revolver, your search is limited to areas where a 357-revolver could be found. The scope of the search is limited. However, if you stated in the affidavit you were searching for 357-caliber bullets, you have broadened your scope and can search where bullets could be found.

Another example might be if you are looking for a stolen 1967 Chevrolet Corvette. If you had sufficient information in your probable cause statement that indicated the car was being dismantled, then you can state you were searching for parts and components of a 1967 Chevrolet Corvette. This focus would certainly broaden your scope because rivets, VIN plates, and other small components could be hidden just about anywhere. The importance of understanding the scope of the search is critical because if you're within the proper scope and discover evidence of other crimes, you can seize that evidence as you go about the search. The first three sections of any search warrant affidavit are simple to write, provided you have the complete information and facts.

The fourth section in a search warrant affidavit is the probable cause statement. This information must be based on facts and circumstances. This section is detailed and sometimes lengthy in order to provide the magistrate with a clear picture of all facts of the investigation. A lot of this information is taken from the reports that you and other officers write. In other words, the information is there to review and transfer to the affidavit.

Once you have completed all the sections, which are usually contained in a template provided by your agency or the magistrate's office, you present the affidavit to the magistrate for consideration. You are placed under oath and swear that the contents of the affidavit are true. I hope your probable cause is sufficient, the warrant is issued, and you recover important evidence.

Years ago, I was involved in an illegal gambling and drug investigation. The base of operations for that illegal activity was in the upstairs room of a local bar. The only way for investigators to access this room was from a fire escape in the rear of the building. The door leading to this room from the outside was a heavy steel door with a deadbolt lock. Based on the investigation, obtaining probable cause to search the room was easy; however, actually getting into the room to search presented a problem. One detective came up with a unique solution. We would make a key. In order to do that, we obtained a search warrant for the inside of the deadbolt lock. Since the door and lock were part of the criminal enterprise, the magistrate issued the warrant. One morning after the business closed, we took a locksmith up the fire escape to the door. In about twenty minutes, we had a key. The next night, we opened the door and walked in.

Discovering evidence of crimes is a critical part of our business that we should take seriously. But it can also be fun.

Memorandum Writing

A memorandum is an internal communication method agencies often use to describe events that have already occurred or that are about to. The word "memorandum" actually means something that should be remembered or kept in mind. For instance, if an employee loses a piece of issued equipment, a memorandum is a way to inform supervisors of the loss. In addition, a supervisor could use a memorandum to sanction the employee for the loss.

Memorandums can call attention to exceptional work done by an employee and often take the form of a written commendation. Agencies deliver notices of official policy changes, upcoming critical events, and other important communications with a memorandum.

Agencies sometimes use their letterhead on the first page of a memorandum. The letterhead is only used on the first page; subsequent pages do not include it. Here are some basic formatting rules to follow in writing memorandums.

The word **MEMORANDUM** should appear at the top of the page, centered or left-aligned. Hit the Enter key twice, so you're two lines down, and write the word **To**, after which you address the intended recipient of the memorandum, giving their full name and title. Below the recipient line is the word **From**, after which you write your name and title. Below this line is the word **Date**, followed by the date on which the memorandum is written. Below the date is the word **Subject**, after which you briefly describe the memorandum's topic. Below is an example of this format.

MEMORANDUM

TO: Roger Smith, Chief
FROM: Beverly Clark, Director of Personnel
DATE: December 2, 2016
SUBJECT: Employee benefits

Memorandums do not begin with a salutation such as "Dear Chief Smith." They should begin with a purpose statement. Examples of words to use in the introductory sentence of a memorandum include *inform, explain, clarify, introduce, provide, commend,* or *notify.* Here are examples of introductory sentences using such words:

The purpose of this memorandum is to <u>notify</u> all employees of a change in the health insurance coverage provided by the city.

The purpose of this memorandum is to <u>inform</u> you of a complaint received concerning your conduct during a traffic stop.

This memorandum will <u>provide</u> you with information concerning the traffic plan for the upcoming festival.

Following the introductory statement comes the body of the memorandum, where the topic is described as briefly as possible. In other words, get to the point. You should close the memorandum using what I call an action plan. Below are examples of statements with an action plan.

All employees should contact the Dir. of Personnel no later than October 4, 2016, in order to register for health insurance.

You are instructed to take greater care to properly maintain your agency issued equipment.

The festival begins at 8:00 a.m. on Friday, and all personnel should report to their assigned stations by 7:45 a.m.

Write memorandums in block style, double-spaced paragraphs. Use one-inch margins at the bottom, left, and right sides. Memorandums do not include a signature line at the bottom. Place your initials by your name in the heading, which indicates you have reviewed and approved the memorandum.

Your agency will determine the form of delivery for memorandums. For information intended for all employees, memorandums are frequently delivered via email. Others are delivered by "hard copy." Below is an example of a complete memorandum.

MEMORANDUM

To: Jerry Harper, Capt. Patrol Division
From: James Roland, Patrol Commander
Date: July 3, 2016
Subject: July 4 Celebration

The purpose of this memorandum is to provide you with details of the upcoming celebration occurring in downtown Knoxville. The Downtown Development Authority has invited several food vendors to participate in this year's celebration and will coordinate their efforts with these vendors. I have been informed that they will set up their trucks along the east side of Main Street beginning at Jefferson Avenue. They will begin serving food at 10:00 a.m. and continue until 6:00 p.m. It is anticipated by the Authority that approximately 5000 people will attend the festival.

All patrol personnel should report to their assigned duty station no later than 8:45 a.m. on July 4 and maintain that position until relieved. Patrol personnel should wear their assigned class B uniform. I will provide you with updates concerning the festival as I receive them.

DISCUSSION TOPIC REVIEW

- Using your reports written in the previous chapters, name three portions that would demonstrate compliance with accreditation and certification standards.
- Review the Undercover Drug Buy Report you wrote. How can the event be used to provide content for a search warrant affidavit?
- Review the search of a car and purse during Scenario 7 in Chapter 7.
- How would the Plain View Doctrine apply to what was seen in the home when officers responded to the domestic dispute?
- What is the difference between an informal email and a memorandum?

Ethics in Writing

CHAPTER 9

DISCUSSION TOPIC

In the 1980's, there ran a cop show called *Hill Street Blues*. It's still around on some channels. Its episodes were set in a fictional police precinct in New York and featured patrol officers, detectives, and supervisors dealing with day-to-day enforcement issues occurring in that city. In one episode, a detective, who was disliked by most in the precinct, confronted a suspect on the street and was later accused of using excessive force in this confrontation. Three other officers were present and saw this altercation. The disliked cop asked the others to write their reports in a way that favored him. They did and turned them into the supervisor of the precinct. The supervisor, who had been on the job for many years, was able to recognize what was going on. He confronted the officers and gave them a chance to rewrite their reports.

Any definition of ethics must include the ability to do the right thing consistently and without favoritism to either side. Through their actions, law enforcement officers in this nation must project and demonstrate honesty, trustworthiness, and professionalism. This behavior must be transparent and open to all scrutiny. These expectations certainly apply to report writing. We gather the facts and document them in our reports fairly and accurately.

Some members in our communities expect police officers to be right all the time. However, police officers are human and make honest mistakes. Do not deliberately make mistakes by knowingly violating internal agency policy and criminal statutes. When bad acts occur, they can never be softened by a passive report. Never go along to get along! As Paul Coelho wrote, *"A mistake repeated more than once is a decision."*

The intentional misrepresentation of the facts, also known as "lying," will usually end your career and can lead to criminal prosecution. It also places a stain on the profession in the public eye and diminishes the confidence communities have in the criminal justice system. Take a look at the articles below regarding the arrest of three police officers for intentionally falsifying reports.

Bayonne cop charged with covering up fellow officer's excessive force

Updated on May 16, 2017 at 10:14 AM Posted on May 15, 2017 at 7:23 PM

Bayonne Police Officer Francis Styles has been charged with falsifying records and "misprision of a felony," authorities said.

By Margaret Schmidt
mschmidt@jjournal.com
The Jersey Journal

A Bayonne police officer lied in an official report to cover up the fact that a fellow officer thrust a foot-long flashlight into a handcuffed suspect's face—an action caught on surveillance video—according to a federal indictment released today.

Officer Francis Styles, 36, of Bayonne, is charged with one count of falsifying records in a federal investigation and one count of "misprision of a felony" for his role in attempting to conceal police brutality by former Bayonne Police Officer

Domenico Lillo, acting U.S. Attorney William E. Fitzpatrick announced this afternoon.

Lillo pleaded guilty a year and a half ago to using excessive force during the 2013 arrest, but his sentencing has been postponed several times. Lillo was also among several cops who were accused in a civil suit of beating two men as they left a Bayonne bar in 2007, a suit the city settled for $100,000.

The indictment against Styles stems from the Dec. 27, 2013, arrest of Brandon Walsh, a Bayonne resident who had an outstanding warrant from Sussex County.

According to today's indictment, Lillo, Styles and an unnamed officer went to Walsh's home on Avenue C to serve the warrant and were unaware that a corner bar had four surveillance cameras rolling that recorded them before and after they arrested and handcuffed Walsh.

"Just before 5 p.m. . . . the video showed defendant Styles and Lillo escorting [Walsh] down an exterior staircase . . . in handcuffs, and taking [him] to the ground," the indictment says. "Styles, Lillo and Officer 1 then brought the handcuffed individual to his feet and escorted [him] toward 53rd Street, with Lillo to the right of [him] and holding [his] right arm, and Officer 1 to the left of [him] holding [his] left arm, and defendant Styles following closely behind."

Walsh was neither struggling nor resisting arrest and wasn't bleeding from his face or head, the indictment said.

The video then showed the officers and Walsh turning the corner from Avenue C onto 53rd Street, the indictment said.

"As they walked toward one of the recording cameras, Lillo looked at what appeared to be a full-sized (i.e., approximately one-foot-long) flashlight in his right hand and thrust the flashlight upwards, intentionally striking Individual's face and causing Individual to double over," the indictment charges.

It continues:

"According to the video recording, Styles was looking directly at Lillo as Lillo struck [Walsh] with the flashlight."

Among his injuries, Walsh sustained a forehead cut that required 15 stitches, the indictment said.

In his report, however, Styles wrote that Walsh violently struggled with the cops and was injured when he hit a wall and the ground outside of his Avenue C home, all of which is false, the indictment said.

If convicted, Styles faces up to 20 years in prison on the falsifying records count and three years on the "misprision of a felony" count, officials said.

Styles' arraignment is pending, officials said.

The case is also the subject of a federal police brutality lawsuit Walsh and members of his family have filed.

Lillo and his wife, Rose, have also pleaded guilty to assisting in the filing of a false report to the U.S. Department of Housing and Urban Development to help a relative fraudulently obtain a federally funded home rehabilitation loan.

https://www.nj.com/hudson/index.ssf/2017/05/bayonne_cop_charged_with_covering_up_fellow_office.html

Fullerton police officer charged with filing false police report

Fullerton Police Officer Miguel Siliceo was charged Wednesday on suspicion of filing a false police report.

By Kelly Puente
kpuente@scng.com
Orange County Register
March 16, 2017 at 7:00 am

FULLERTON – A Fullerton police officer has been accused of filing a false police report after he stated that a suspect resisted arrest when police body camera footage showed otherwise, authorities said.

Miguel Siliceo, 51, of Anaheim was charged Wednesday with one felony count of false report by a peace officer. If convicted, he faces up to three years in jail, according to the Orange County District Attorney's Office.

Prosecutors said Siliceo was on patrol with his partner in downtown Fullerton on July 9, 2015, when he arrested a man, identified only as John Doe, for resisting arrest.

Siliceo prepared an arrest report stating that the man "charged at Siliceo's partner during the arrest of another suspect," prosecutors said.

The DA's Office said it relied on Siliceo's report when it charged the man with one misdemeanor count of resisting arrest.

Prosecutors later reviewed body camera footage from other officers at the scene and determined that the footage did not corroborate Siliceo's arrest report, the DA's Office said. Prosecutors dropped charges against the man and filed criminal charges against Siliceo.

The DA investigated this case with the "full cooperation" of the Fullerton Police Department, authorities said.

Fullerton Police Department spokeswoman Sgt. Kathryn Hamel said Siliceo was placed on paid administrative leave in October, pending the investigation. The department is in the process of an internal affairs review and declined to comment further on the case, she said.

Siliceo was one of a group of Fullerton officers honored by the county and Mothers Against Drunk Driving in 2015 for making more than three dozen DUI arrests.

Prosecutors said they may seek to introduce evidence regarding Siliceo's conduct in filing a false insurance claim in 1999.

He is scheduled to be arraigned April 5.

https://www.ocregister.com/2017/03/16/fullerton-police-officer-charged-with-filing-false-police-report/

Ex-Baldwin Park cop charged with filing false report on drug arrest

Ex-Baldwin Park police officer Matt DeHoog, wearing No. 57, is seen during the National Public Safety Football League game between the Southern California Strikeforce and the Ventura County Hogs at Baldwin Park High School on April 2, 2011. DeHoog has been charged with filing a false police report related to a drug arrest.

By Brian Day
San Gabriel Valley Tribune
Posted: 02/20/14, 3:18 PM PST | Updated: on 02/20/2014

LOS ANGELES >> Prosecutors Thursday filed a felony charge against a former Baldwin Park police officer accused of filing a false police report related to a drug arrest last year.

Matthew DeHoog, 29, pleaded not guilty to a count of filing a false report in Los Angeles Superior Court, Los Angeles County District Attorney's officials said in a written statement. Judge Renee Korn ordered him released on his own recognizance pending his next court appearance.

"DeHoog wrote a false police report about a July 31, 2013 incident where a man was arrested for investigation of possession of methamphetamine," according to the district attorney's office statement.

The criminal complaint filed against DeHoog alleges that, while working as a police officer, he filed a report regarding the commission and investigation of a crime, "and knowingly and intentionally included a statement and statements regarding a material matter which the defendant knew to be false."

But further details regarding the alleged false police report, including the identity of the man who was arrested, were not available.

"We're not releasing any more facts of the case," district attorney's office spokesman Greg Risling said. "They'll be released during the [preliminary hearing]."

The case was investigated by DeHoog's former colleagues at the Baldwin Park Police Department. But police also declined to discuss the circumstances of the case.

"He's a former police officer with our department and he's no longer employed by us," Baldwin Park Police Chief Michael Taylor said.

DeHoog's employment with the department ended in early January, Taylor said, however a specific time frame was not immediately available.

The chief said he had no further comment regarding the allegations against the former officer, or the case filed Thursday by the district attorney's office.

"It's unfortunate when anything like this happens in the law enforcement community," Taylor said.

DeHoog was ordered to return to court March 4 for a preliminary hearing setting, Risling said.

DeHoog could not be reached for comment Thursday.

Under state law, DeHoog faces up to three years in prison if convicted as charged.

https://www.sgvtribune.com/2014/02/20/ex-baldwin-park-cop-charged-with-filing-false-report-on-drug-arrest/

In today's unsettled environment, seen playing across televisions throughout the nation, some police officers become conflicted over their role. Ordered to stand down at the site of protesters burning their police cars and looting local businesses has to be difficult. Hesitating to take the proper action for fear it will make the lead story on the nightly news broadcast has become an unfortunate consideration. Some officers have left the profession entirely, and agency recruitment efforts have suffered.

Despite these difficulties, those in this profession—and those looking to join—must be honest. You must practice honesty each day in what you do and write about. The International Association of Chiefs of Police has developed and distributed a code of ethics for law enforcement that sums up our expectations in this regard.

Law Enforcement Code of Ethics

As a law enforcement officer, my fundamental duty is to serve the community; to safeguard lives and property; to protect the innocent against deception, the weak against oppression or intimidation and the peaceful against violence or disorder; and to respect the constitutional rights of all to liberty, equality, and justice.

> I will keep my private life unsullied as an example to all and will behave in a manner that does not bring discredit to me or to my agency. I will maintain courageous calm in the face of danger, scorn or ridicule; develop self-restraint; and be constantly mindful of the welfare of others. Honest in thought and deed both in my personal and official life, I will be exemplary in obeying the law and the regulations of my department. Whatever I see or hear of a confidential nature or that is confided to me in my official capacity will be kept ever secret unless revelation is necessary in the performance of my duty.
>
> I will never act officiously or permit personal feelings, prejudices, political beliefs, aspirations, animosities or friendships to influence my decisions. With no compromise for crime and with relentless prosecution of criminals, I will enforce the law courteously and appropriately without fear or favor, malice or ill will, never employing unnecessary force or violence and never accepting gratuities.
>
> I recognize the badge of my office as a symbol of public faith, and I accept it as a public trust to be held so long as I

am true to the ethics of police service. I will never engage in acts of corruption or bribery, nor will I condone such acts by other police officers. I will cooperate with all legally authorized agencies and their representatives in the pursuit of justice.

I know that I alone am responsible for my own standard of professional performance and will take every reasonable opportunity to enhance and improve my level of knowledge and competence.

I will constantly strive to achieve these objectives and ideals, dedicating myself before God to my chosen profession . . . law enforcement.

A Look Back

We have covered a lot of ground in our mission to write better police reports. We have discussed the importance of reports and their impact on the criminal justice system. They document important facts about events occurring in our neighborhoods and criminal activity that may put us all in danger.

Suspense novels intentionally misdirect readers who find out that what they thought to be true was not. Our reports can't mislead or misdirect. We collect information in various ways, then write "just the facts" about what we learn. We must be clear; therefore, we cannot leave room for our personal interpretations of these facts. Rarely are our opinions appropriate in police reports.

Some facts about criminal activity are reported to the FBI and analyzed. They publish an annual report using this data to track crime trends across the United States. Police agencies frequently use this information to enhance enforcement activities and even budget requests.

In addition to the FBI and police agencies, our reports reach an unlimited amount of readers. Prosecutors, supervisors, judges, lawyers, private citizens, and even members of the media can look at our reports. Sometimes, they end up on the front page of newspapers and on the Internet. That is why we should strive to make our reports something to be proud of and not a source of embarrassment. They really are a reflection of our agency and ourselves.

By now, you have developed your own unique style of note-taking and understand that every good report starts with good notes. I hope that you have a list of supplies that you plan to buy to prepare for your first report. And I hope you remember the organizational tips we've discussed.

Police agencies across the nation develop forms they use based on their specific needs. They design their report writing software within records management systems to enhance their officers' ability to complete reports efficiently. Formatting will vary between agencies with the use of first-person vs. third-person sentences and of military vs. civilian times. It's good to remember how to use both.

Collecting content about an event is critical. Reports that do not tell the complete story using the 4W+H elements serve no purpose. Even though some of this information may not be available at the time, the report should use the 4W+H elements to piece out the most complete story possible. Think back on the reports you have written. The victim of the stolen lawnmower established the time frame the theft occurred. The neighbor was able to give a glimpse of who stole the lawnmower by the description they gave. Investigators going room to room searching and discovering drug evidence and the crime scene investigator describing the conditions and evidence found at the death scene are examples of some of these important elements.

Carefully proofreading our reports before submitting them is also important. They should be both factually and grammatically correct. Remembering some basic punctuation and spelling rules will help ensure good-quality reports. You will find yourself using a lot of the same words in each of your reports, so learn how to use them properly. The same goes for punctuation. You should also remember the software (sometimes preloaded on computers) and how it can aid in discovering some common spelling, punctuation, and word choice errors.

A large number of police agencies have striven to become better by implementing policies and procedures to improve not only their reputation, but also their quality of service. National accreditation and state certification are becoming the norm. Police reports serve as the basis for which agencies can achieve compliance.

Another general agency practice is using memorandums as a formal means of internal communication. All memorandums are generally formatted in the same way, but they are used for many purposes. Remember, memorandums get to the point and may not be lengthy at all. The introductory sentence, the body, and an action plan make up a good memorandum.

Another important document to write well is the search warrant affidavit. They are one of the most important documents that detectives write. To establish probable cause, affidavits combine most of the information a detective collected and documented throughout a criminal investigation. In fact, officers sometimes use computer-formatting tools to cut and paste content from actual reports into affidavits. These documents must fulfill important legal requirements.

All documents you write reflect your honesty in your police activities. Never let circumstances influence the way in which you write about them. People recognize a simple mistake, but when you try to try to soften that mistake through false reporting, you always make things worse. Writing false reports is a crime and a character flaw that cannot be tolerated in this profession. It is a career-ender.

In my criminal investigation courses preparing students for a career in law enforcement, the theme is "leave no stone unturned." Run every lead, talk to every witness, and use all technology that's available to solve the crime. Never give up and always look for things you might have missed. Consult colleagues and partners, and at the end of the investigation, be satisfied that you have looked under every stone for clues. Some people believe a criminal investigation is only a success if someone is arrested and convicted for the crime. I disagree. We are seeing more cold case squads being developed to look at unsolved cases. Of course, the first thing investigators do is pull the investigative file, which contains all of the reports written during the earlier investigation sometimes years earlier. They search the file to make sure all the leads were followed and witnesses were interviewed. If the reports were not complete and do not contain the 4W+H elements and the details they require, then the cases remain unsolved. However, if all the information is there and tells the complete story, then the report can allow the cold case investigator to gain new insight into what happened. These cases are often solved because technology now exists that was not available at the time. The earlier investigators did a good job collecting and documenting evidence, which can now be examined further. Even though no arrest was made at the time of the original investigation, if the officers did a thorough job as reflected in their reports, they can lead the new investigators to the offender.

When asked what it feels like to win, most people reflect about a sporting event in high school, an election, or maybe a winning lottery ticket. For police officers, winning may take other forms. Catching the bank robber in a foot chase, finding the lost child who's been missing overnight, getting the confession from a serial killer, and safely going home to families at the end of a shift are all wins. The ability for police officers to properly collect and document information in reports is also a win: a win for them, their agencies, and the communities where they live and work. So why not write to win—to protect and serve.

Glossary

Grammar Terms

Some officers write lengthy reports using unnecessary words. They think their phrases are more formal, while some even believe using "fancy" words makes them look smarter. Our reports should use common, everyday words that are understood by everyone and need no explanation. The following is a list of such unnecessary words or phrases that frequently appear in less than effective police reports. Using the substitute words in parenthesis can improve your report writing.

Accumulate (gather)

Advise (inform)

A limited quantity of (few)

Altercation (fight)

Answer in the affirmative (say yes)

Anticipate (foresee)

Applicable (applied to)

Ascertain (find out)

As per (according to)

At a later date (later)

At the present time (now)

Attached you will find (attached is)

Attribute (due)

Close proximity (near)

Commence (start)

Demonstrate (show)

During the course of (during)

Encounter (meet)

Exit (leave or get out of)

Expedite (hurry)

Facilitate (simplify, make easy)

Finalize (finish, end)

For the purpose of (for, to)

Frequently (often)

In a timely manner (promptly)

In order to (to)

In regard to (concerning)

In relation to (about)

In the vicinity of (near)

Is as follows (follows)

Locate (find, put)

Make a determination (determined)

Observed (saw)

Obtained (get, got)

Participate (take part)

Prior to (before)

Proceed (go)

Procure (get)

Residence (house, apartment, mobile home)

Terminated (ended, stopped)

Transported (drove, took)

Vehicle (car, truck, motorhome, etc.)

Without further delay (soon, quickly)

The English language has many words similar in sound but different in spelling and meaning. These are called homophones, and you should watch out for them. Some words are not exact homophones but are near enough in sound—though not in use—to cause confusion. Be sure to use the word you mean. Below are a few examples:

Already (by this or a specified time)

When I arrived at the scene, the ambulance was already there.

All ready (all things are ready)

The SWAT team was <u>all ready</u> to enter the home.

Brake (stopping and the pedal in a car)

The <u>brake</u> pedal failed to engage.

Break (shatter or separate)

The fire department had to <u>break</u> in the burning car.

Canvas (a heavy, coarse fabric)

He painted on a blue <u>canvas</u>.

Canvass (to examine thoroughly, to solicit)

We conducted a neighborhood <u>canvass</u>.

Council (a body of people elected by voters)

I appeared before the City <u>Council</u>.

Counsel (consultation or a lawyer)

The defendant appeared in court represented by <u>counsel</u>.

Die (to stop living)

The doctor told the family members their loved one was going to <u>die</u>.

Dye (a colored substance that has an affinity to the substrate to which it is being applied)

The bank robber told the teller not to include a <u>dye</u>-pack with the money.

Farther (beyond; relates to distance)

The wreck occurred farther down the road.

Further (additional, more)

The prosecutor stated he had no further questions.

Here (location)

<u>Here</u> is the spot where the body was found.

Hear (listen)

The witness said she could <u>hear</u> gunshots.

Hours (time)

The police department is open twenty-four <u>hours</u> a day.

Ours (ownership by two or more people)

The red Corvette is <u>ours</u>.

Imminent (likely to occur)

It seemed a fight was imminent.

Eminent (respected, outstanding)

Officer Jones was an eminent detective.

Lie (resting, sleeping, and napping)

The patient was asked to lie down.

Lay (when placing something)

Inmate Jones was told to lay down his weapon.

Lose (misplace)

If you lose your handcuffs, you must reimburse the department.

Loose (not tight)

The inmate escaped because the handcuffs were too loose.

One (the number; singular)

One of our officers was hurt in the wreck.

Won (past tense of win)

Billy won the top gun award at the firing range.

Past (no longer current)

Past behavior is a good predictor of future behavior.

Passed (to move on ahead, proceed)

The blue car passed the intersection rapidly.

Principal (director of a school)

Johnny was asked to see the principal at the elementary school.

Principle (an amount of money that has been borrowed or invested, also means important)

The mortgage required Jason to repay the principle amount of the loan first.

Personal (private or intimate)

Some personal clothing of the victim was taken in the burglary.

Personnel (employees)

All personnel was accounted for.

Piece (a part of)

A piece of the tail section of the airplane was recovered in the road.

Peace (calm)

The mother of the gunshot victim was at peace.

Quiet (not noisy)

The burglar was quiet.

Quite ("rather" or "very")

The homeowner was quite anxious to see the officer arrive.

Set (to put into position)

Set the tripod in the middle of the road.

Sit (to be seated)

The spectators were asked to sit in the folding chairs.

Stationary (not moving, not capable of being moved)

The surveillance team took up a stationary position.

Stationery (writing paper)

> *I ordered some <u>stationery</u> with the agency letterhead.*

Trusty (an inmate worker in prison or jail)

> *A <u>trusty</u> at the Sheriff's Office washed my car.*

Trustee (a person or agent in a position of trust)

> *The <u>trustee</u> of the estate was John Smith.*

To (indicates direction or purpose)

> *The officer gave directions <u>to</u> the motorist.*

Too (excessive or also)

> *Barbara Jones was charged with driving <u>too</u> fast for conditions.*

Two (a number)

> *There were <u>two</u> cars involved in the accident.*

Their (refers to ownership by two or more people)

> *The inmates were ordered to take <u>their</u> shoes off.*

There (is an adverb describing a place)

> *<u>There</u> is a good place to eat across town.*

They're (another way to write "they are")

> *<u>They're</u> waiting on the ambulance.*

Than (a comparison word)

It's easier to walk <u>than</u> to run.

Then (a time word)

The detective fired one shot, <u>then</u> he drove away.

Week (seven-day period)

The package will be delivered in one <u>week</u>

Weak (lacking in strength)

The loss of blood made the victim <u>weak</u>.

Another mistake occurring frequently in police reports is the misuse of the words *gone* and *went*. *Went* is the past tense of *go*. *Gone* is the past participle of *go*. If you're not sure whether to use *gone* or *went*, remember that *gone* always needs words like *has, have, had, is, am, are, was, were,* and *be* before it, but *went* doesn't. For example:

He had went to the store earlier. Incorrect. Should be *He went to the store earlier.*

He had gone to the store earlier. Correct.

Jargon

External reports—reports which describe incidents in the field and are used by multiple departments, including in the public (Chapter 1).

File numbers—the unique number issues to each case (Chapter 4).

Freedom of Information Act (FOIA)—federal law that allows full or partial public disclosure of documents held by the federal government (Chapter 3).

Index crimes—crimes that are critical to track, as determined by the International Association of Chiefs of Police. Divided into Part I, the eight most serious crimes, and Part II, twenty-one less commonly reported crimes (Chapter 2).

Internal reports—reports used within the police force, usually for administrative reasons (Chapter 1).

Open records laws—records and documents that are available to the public upon request. The documents considered public vary in each state (Chapter 3).

Uniform Crime Report Program (UCR)—official crime report data collectively gathered by law enforcement agencies across the United States (Chapter 2).

References

Day, B. (2014, February 20). *Ex-Baldwin Park cop charged with filing a false report on drug arrest.* San Gabriel Valley Tribune. Retrieved from http:/www.sgvtribune.com

Davis, J. N., & Kam, R. V. (2008). *Report writing for criminal justice professionals: A complete text from English composition to interviews and investigations.* San Clemente, CA: LawTech Custom Publishing Co., Inc.

Frazee, B., & Davis, J. N. (2009). *Painless police report writing: An English guide for criminal Justice professionals* (3rd Ed.). Upper Saddle River, NJ: Pearson Education, Inc.

Goodman-Lerner, D. J. (2015). *Report it in writing* (6th Ed.). New York, NY: Pearson Education, Inc.

Ga. Association of Chiefs of Police. (2016). *State Certification.* Retrieved from http:/www.gachiefs.com/index.php/state certification

Ga. Bureau of Investigation. (2014). *Investigative file 08-0089-01-2014.* Cleveland, GA: Region 8 field office.

International Association of Chiefs of Police. (2017). *Ethics Toolkit.* Retrieved from http:/www.theiacp.org/ethics

Miller, L. S., & Whitehead, J. T. (2015). *Report writing for criminal justice professionals* (5th Ed.). Boston, MA: Elsevier, Inc.

Puente, K. (2017, March 16). *Fullerton police officer charged with filing false report.* Orange County Register. Retrieved from http:/www.ocregister.com

Reynolds, J. (2011). *The criminal justice report writing guide for officers.* Lexington, KY: The Maple Leaf Press.

Schmidt, M. (2007, May 16). *Bayonne cop charged with covering up fellow officer's excessive force.* The Jersey Journal. Retrieved from http:/www.nj.com/journal

Scalise, F., & Strosahl, D. (2013). *A street officer's guide to report writing.* Clifton Park, NY: Delmar, Cengage Learning.

The Commission on Accreditation for Law enforcement. (2017) *Law Enforcement Accreditation.* Gainesville, Va.

United States Constitution. Retrieved June 27, 2017, from http:/ enwilipedia.org/wiki:/united_states_constitution

Webb, J. (Writer, Director). (1953). "The Big Thief" [Television series episode]. In J. Webb (Producer), *Dragnet.* U.S.A.: Mark VII, Ltd.

CPSIA information can be obtained
at www.ICGtesting.com
Printed in the USA
BVHW062215160120
569709BV00006B/82